序　言

　　China News 和 China Post 是國內最普及的英文報紙，報導內容也和國人息息相關，讀者除了可以從中汲取包羅萬象的最新訊息，更能學到最正確、實用的英文，甚至道地的英文表達和幽默。所以，看英文報紙是學英文最方便、最便宜、最有效的途徑。

　　「如何看懂 China Post & China News」告訴您迅速看懂英文報紙的訣竅，讓您認識新聞英語標題，熟悉文章體裁，更告訴您如何不查字典便能看懂生字，並配合練習題，使您完全熟悉新聞英語的特色。

　　本書精選 China News 和 China Post 精彩文章，共分為社會文化、政治軍事、體育娛樂、生活醫藥、經濟貿易及社論專欄六大類。每篇文章後，皆有精心設計的測驗題，訓練您的閱讀理解力，並附上詳盡的翻譯及註釋，使您在短時間內融會貫通，學會活的英文。

　　書中附有英文報紙各版常見字彙、精彩的分類廣告詞彙、國內各媒體中英名稱、我國及美國政府機構、美國五十州及首府和世界各國及首都的中英名稱。且本書版面參照英文報紙設計，更可增加閱讀的真實感。

　　本書編譯及版面均力求完善，但錯失之處，恐所不免，衷心祈望各界讀者不吝指正批評，愚編幸甚。

編者　謹識

C·O·N·T·E·N·T·S

C·O·N·T·E·N·T·S

China News 「英文中國日報」

China News 於民國四十年創刊，其版面清爽、作風嚴謹。各版主要內容如下：

第一版為國際政治重大新聞；第二、三版為 Local（地方新聞）；第四版為 Asia／Pacific（亞太新聞）；第五版為 Americas（美洲新聞）；第六版為 Europe／Africa（歐洲／非洲新聞）；第七版為 Opinion（社論）；第八、九版為 Business（經貿新聞）；第十版為 Classified ADS（分類廣告）；第十一版為 Entertainment／Leisure（娛樂休閒）；第十二版為 Sports（體育新聞）。

週五並附有 Weekend 專刊，告訴你台灣最佳的娛樂、餐飲去處。週日的學生專刊更是在學生充電的利器。

China Post 「中國郵報」

China Post 於民國四十一年創刊，版面活潑，內容多彩多姿：第一版為國際政治重大新聞；第二版為 International News（國際新聞）；第三版為 The Americas（美洲新聞）；第四版為 Commentary（社論）。

自第五版以後，版面內容極富變化，包括 Around the World（世界珍聞）、Sports（運動新聞）、Arts & Leisure（藝術休閒）、Business（經濟新聞）、以及醫療、教育、科技新知等，更有豐富的分類廣告和完備的飛機時刻表，週五並有餐飲旅遊專刊，週日有廣受學生歡迎的 The Student Post。

U.S. **Part 1**

英文報紙閱讀訣竅

新聞英語標題

時代社會瞬息萬變，人們生活多元化且複雜化，再加上日新月異的科技，使我們能很快地獲得全球各地最新消息，因此，報紙的頁數便大大增加了。就台灣而言，自報禁解除後，國內報紙由三大張最多增加到了十二大張之多。而以美國報紙的週日版來說，一、兩百頁早已不足為奇了。報紙頁數的增加，使許多忙碌的現代人，每日看報紙只讀標題，因此，標題的作用及重要性，也相對提高了。

◎ 標題要能吸引讀者的注意力

報紙的標題猶如商店的櫥窗，展示的商品吸引人，顧客才會上門。因此，標題要以簡潔的文字道出全文重點，並利用文字押韻、排比、對仗或影射等技巧，使讀者有興趣閱讀內容。

◎ 標題的位置及大小，表示新聞的重要程度

重要新聞需要強調，運用大字號或大篇幅，吸引注意力。英文報紙中，通常右欄上段是當天頭條新聞，其次是左欄上段、及中上方。

▶ 掌握基本原則便能看懂標題 ◀

一、主題字的彰顯與字的省略

　　前面提過，爲了要吸引讀者注意，標題用字力求簡潔有力與醒目，往往只用一些主題字或表達上不可或缺的字。請看下列實例解析：

Taiwan-born college student
sentenced to life by U.S. court

⇨ *A* Taiwan-born college student *was* sentenced to life by U.S. court.

（台籍大學生被美法院判無期徒刑。）

* sentence〔ˈsɛntəns〕*v.* 判刑

　　前例一開頭省略了不定冠詞 a，但如果不定冠詞表 one 的意味，則不可省略。be 動詞 was 也被省略，直接用過去分詞表示被動。〔注意：標題中的 be 動詞幾乎都被省略。〕

二、動詞時式的問題

　　由於篇幅和表現法的關係，新聞報導文體和一般文學作品截然不同。尤其是標題用字更要濃縮，故其句子的時態與動詞問題發展出了慣用的一套。由下列實例中，可見一斑。

Man-made quake *damages* homes

（人爲地震破壞家園。）

在標題中，一般剛發生或最近的過去時態，都使用現在式。其目的是要彰顯新聞的新鮮感。值得注意的是，不定詞 to 也廣泛地用於標題中表示未來式：

Saudis *to* keep extra oil output
（沙烏地將繼續增產石油。）

* Saudi〔səˈudɪ〕*n.* 沙烏地阿拉伯人
  output〔ˈaut,put〕*n.* 產量

句中的 to 即表示了「將行～」或「準備要做～」。

三、標點符號的運用

以標點符號來代替某些單字，是使標題內容精簡的常用途徑。例如，逗號「，」常用來代替對等連接詞 and：

Woman kills husband, self
（婦人殺夫並自盡。）

標題中的冒號「：」通常表示消息來源或內容：

N. Korea : War clouds over peninsula
（北韓表示將出兵南韓半島。）

* peninsula〔pəˈnɪnsələ〕*n.* 半島

〔注意：有時冒號後的內容是對前面的說明加以補充。〕

分號「；」用來分隔獨立的子句，表示標題中包含了兩件事：

Fire strikes hospital ; 2 dead
（醫院大火；兩人死亡）

解答☞ p. 265

試著將下列標題,改寫成完整的英文句子:

1. ROC not likely to be targeted

   ⇨
   _____

2. Chief absent from meeting on defense

   ⇨
   _____

3. Ozone layer thinner over Europe

   ⇨
   _____

4. Europe teams to face the heat

   ⇨
   _____

5. Former university teacher arrested

   ⇨
   _____

新聞英語文章

新聞寫作最重傳達眞實報導，因此，寫作技巧非常重要。一位總編曾說過：「没有平凡的新聞，祇有平凡的記者。」（There are no dull stories, only dull reporters.）因此，新聞文章的好壞，取決於記者的寫作技巧。許多有名的作家，如史蒂芬‧克蘭（Stephen Crane）、馬克‧吐溫（Mark Twain）及海明威（Ernest Hemingway）等，都是由新聞記者做起，最後寫作技巧臻至完美。在文章結構方面，近年來，爲了吸引讀者興趣，除了記者奉爲圭臬的「倒金字塔式」外，更發展出不同種類的文體，如敍事體（The narrative approach）、因人敍事體（The personalized approach）及編年體（The chronological approach）等等。眞可謂之百家爭鳴，而讀者更可欣賞各種文體，享受閱報的樂趣。

🔯 好的新聞文章具有五個因素：

　1. 精確（precise）

　2. 明白（clear）

　3. 步調（pace）合其內容

　4. 用轉折布局（transitional devices）引人入勝

　5. 訴諸讀者感受（senses）

▶三全其美的倒金字塔式◀

　　「倒金字塔式」（The inverted pyramid approach）使所報導的事實按輕重先後，做層次分明的表現，是最能表現新聞精神的文體，能讓讀者看到最需要知道的訊息，後面的細節詳述，若不感興趣，可隨時打住，而仍能了解新聞梗概。此外，這種寫作方式使印刷和新聞編輯更為方便，真可謂之三全其美。

一、導言是新聞的提綱和精華

　　導言是讀者最急於知道的事實，在一、兩句中，包括了一個事件最重要的，最新的發展或最後的結果。包含了誰（who）、何事（what）、何時（when）、何地（where）、原因（why）及情況（how）。讀完了導言，便能滿足好奇心，瞭解整個事件。例如：

　　A former police officer in White Plains, N.Y. who robbed a liquor store to help pay US $ 200,000 medical bills for his brain-damaged 4-year-old son was spared prison recently.

　　（一位曾任職於紐約州白平原市的警官，為了要替他腦部受傷的四歲兒子付二十萬美金的醫藥費，而搶劫一家酒店。最近，他被判免於牢獄之災。）

　**　former〔ˊfɔrmɚ〕*adj.* 以前的　　rob〔rɑb〕*v.* 搶劫
　　　liquor〔ˊlɪkɚ〕*n.* 烈酒　　bill〔bɪl〕*n.* 帳單
　　　spare〔spɛr〕*v.* 赦免

> **who** : a former police officer
>
> **what** : was spared prison
>
> **when** : recently
>
> **where** : White Plains, N.Y.
>
> **why** : to help pay medical bills
>
> **how** : robbed a liquor store

二、句法簡潔流暢

　　新聞寫作中的句法，除了精確外，還要流暢，使讀者容易瞭解。通常，用短而多起伏的句子表達動作、緊張或變化，長句子則可使步調趨於緩進。轉折可幫助讀者抓住新聞。在不同的段落中，沒有不必要的重覆，更吸引讀者一口氣讀到底。

 一分鐘內閱讀下題導言並作答：　　　　　　　解答 ☞ ₚ. 265

■ The Council of Agriculture yesterday unveiled plans to increase its manpower and coordinate efforts to entirely stop the illegal trade in endangered species within three to six years.

This article is about :

(A) the development of agriculture.

(B) a plan of protecting endangered species.

(C) how to encourage international trade.

(D) how to stop illegal agricultural production.

新聞英語字彙

寫作的基礎，是一個個的單字，新聞文章也是一樣，用字要謹慎，才能傳遞眞實訊息，又能吸引讀者閱讀意願。西方作家常有這樣的建議：「使用一個字之前，你要把它拉一拉，試試它的靭性；把它摔到地上去，試試它的強度。」這無非是強調寫作時用字要經過不斷的嚴格訓練，才能寫出適當又易懂的字詞。至於俚語（ slang ），美聯社認爲：「在新聞報導中，俚語少用爲妙。」尤其是具有侮辱性的俚語，記者都會避免。如稱警察爲 cops，水手爲 gobs，中國人爲 Chin，義大利人爲 Wops。

§ 好的寫作，就是把意思縮短，用短的字代替長的字，用單字代替片語，言簡意賅。

§ 英國詩人柯爾雷基（ Samuel T. Coleridge ）論詩，說它是「最好的字以最好的順序排列」，新聞文章也是一樣，我們可以從中學到高層次而活用的英文。

§ 新聞英語中的字彙是比較容易讀得出來的字、比較容易寫得出來的字、和比較容易瞭解的字。

▶不查字典也能看懂文章◀

　　對於初學閱讀英文報紙的人來說，不認識的單字往往是最頭痛的事，查字典次數太頻繁，會中斷閱讀及思緒，更會降低閱讀興趣而感到厭倦。其實，看到不懂的單字，不需要立即打開字典。在查字典前，不妨先試試以下方法：

一、尋找同位語或解釋

　　新聞英語文章中，通常是英語系國民較容易瞭解的字；若非得使用職業術語（ jargon ）或行話（ shoptalk ）時，也會在文中加以註解，例如：

　　　　A *doubloon*, one of the first gold coins minted in the United States, was sold Friday for an apparent world record price of 430,000.

　　　　（一枚西班牙金幣——美國最早鑄造的金幣之一——週五以四十三萬元的高價賣出，破了世界紀錄。）

　　** doubloon〔dʌ'blun〕*n.* 昔西班牙之金幣名　　mint〔mɪnt〕*v.* 鑄造

　　上句中，*doubloon* 是比較困難的字，但我們可由同位語one of the first gold coins minted in the United States,判斷出它是一種古老的金幣。

二、由上下文猜測單字意義

　　若句中遇到不懂的單字很少，則可由上下文及句子來判斷生字的意思，例如：

A Chinese couple, flying low to *evade* radar
controls, escaped to the West Friday in a crop-
dusting aircraft, police said.

（警方表示，一對中國夫妻週五駕駛一架噴灑農藥機，
逃到西方國家，他們低空飛行以躲避雷達的偵察。）

** evade〔ɪ'ved〕*v.* 躲避　　radar〔'redɑr〕*n.* 雷達
crop-dusting〔'krɑp,dʌstɪŋ〕*n.*（從低飛的飛機上）噴灑農藥

如果你能想到這對夫妻低空飛行和雷達偵測的關係，你就
會知道句中 evade 的意思了。

三、尋找同義字

在新聞報導中，與主題相關的字往往會出現很多次，但如
果反覆使用同一字，會使全文枯燥乏味。因此，文章中都盡量
避免使用同一個字，若能留心文中的同義字，便能輕鬆理解生
字意義。例如：

In a new twist to a recent flurry of *espionage*
cases, a German male worker appeared in court on
spying charges.

（最近一連串的德國間諜案中，又有了意外的發展——
一名德國郵局男性員工因從事間諜活動，而出庭應訊。）

** flurry〔'flɝɪ〕*n.* 混亂　　espionage〔,ɛspɪə'nɑʒ〕*n.* 間諜行為

上句中，我們可從 *spying* 推敲出 *espionage* 的意思，如
此一來，即使不查字典也能了解單字的意義了。

解答☞ p. 265

由上下文來判斷斜體字的意思，並選出其同義字詞：

1. Many Americans favor the *flogging* of a U.S. teenager who destroyed cars. A boy from Dayton, Ohio, was sentenced to six strokes of a rattan cane.
   (A) killing   (B) beating
   (C) laughing   (D) praising

2. The peace talks have reached a *deadlock* ; both South Korea and North Korea are not willing to compromise.
   (A) true worth
   (B) hatred
   (C) failure to reach agreement
   (D) error statement

3. Full-time housewives represented only 31.3 percent of women over the age of 15, a decline of 0.7 percent over the 1982 figure. The decline reflected the increasing number of housewives aged 35 to 44 who sought full-time or part-time jobs to *augment* family income.
   (A) increase   (B) decrease
   (C) stop   (D) practice

Part 2

Society & Culture 社會文化

Transportation *Friday Jan. 21*

New highway policy to be adopted

Compiled by The China Post

Transportation and Communications Minister Liu Chao-shiuan apologized for the New Year highway jams yesterday and revealed plans to regulate vehicles using the national freeway around Lunar New Year.

Liu said the ministry is developing a new policy to allow only vehicles carrying at least four passengers to use the Sun Yat-sen Freeway during the coming holidays early next month.

About 1.29 million vehicles, roughly a 55 percent increase over normal traffic, used the freeway during the Jan. 1-3 holiday.

The ministry has managed the entrance of vehicles onto the freeway with ramps and free use of the freeway during midnight hours to ease daytime jams during consecutive holidays.

解答☞ p. 265

1. What will the new policy be ?
   (A) Only 4-wheel drive vehicles will be allowed.
   (B) No trucks will be allowed on the freeways.
   (C) Only cars with 4 passengers will be allowed.
   (D) Only special registration vehicles will be allowed in the 4 day period.

2. What happened during the holiday period?
   (A) There was a 55% increase in vehicles to 1.29 million.
   (B) There was a 55% increase in vehicles from the usual 1.29 million.
   (C) There was a 55% increase in vehicles from the last New Year.
   (D) There was a 55% increase in the number of vehicles carrying 4 passengers.

3. How has the ministry managed the use of vehicles onto the freeway ?
   (A) By encouraging off-peak use of the freeway and controlled access.
   (B) By restricting access to ramps and nighttime use.
   (C) By requiring cars to carry four passengers.
   (D) By easing daytime jams during consecutive holidays.

高速公路新政策即將採行

交通部長劉兆玄昨天爲新年期間高速公路阻塞的情況向民衆致歉。並且透露，在農曆年期間，計劃管制車輛行駛高速公路。

劉部長指出，交通部正在研擬一項新的政策，在下個月初的假期中，只允許坐滿四人以上的車輛行駛中山高速公路。

在一月一日至三日的假期中，約有一百廿九萬部車輛行駛高速公路，交通流量比平時增加55％。

交通部已經採用匝道管制的方式，調節高速公路的車流量，並且實施夜間免收費的方式，以紓解連續假日白天交通擁塞的情況。

** highway 〔'haɪˌwe〕 n. 高速公路　　adopt 〔ə'dɑpt〕 v. 採用
Transportation and Communication Minister　交通部長
jam 〔dʒæm〕 n. 阻塞　　regulate 〔'rɛgjəˌlet〕 v. 調整
vehicle 〔'viɪkl̩〕 n. 車輛　　Lunar New Year　農曆新年
ministry 〔'mɪnɪstrɪ〕 n. 部　　roughly 〔'rʌflɪ〕 adv. 大約地
ramp 〔ræmp〕 n. 坡道
consecutive 〔kən'sɛkjətɪv〕 adj. 連續的

Family

Pope says families have a peace duty

Vatican City—Pope John Paul stressed on Sunday that families around the world had a duty to work for peace and said husbands and wives must stay together and respect life from the moment of conception. "The family...holds within itself the future of society," the 73-year-old Pontiff said in his weekly Angelus message delivered to the faithful in St. Peter's Square.

The Roman Catholic Church and the United Nations have declared 1994 the International Year of the Family, and the Church has drawn up a charter promoting the rights of parents and their children. The Year of the Family was officially inaugurated Sunday with a mass in Nazareth, in the Holy Land, where according to the Bible Mary and Joseph raised Jesus Christ.

解答☞ p. 265

1. Pope John Paul emphasized the importance of
   (A) stress.　　　(B) families around the world.
   (C) duty.　　　 (D) working.

2. What does the future of society depend on?
   (A) the family 　　(B) the Angelus
   (C) the faithful 　(D) the pontiff

教宗指出：家庭有促進和平之責任

　　梵蒂岡城電——教宗若望·保羅星期天強調，全世界的家庭都有義務努力促進和平，而且丈夫和妻子必須生活在一起，自懷孕那時起，就應尊重生命。七十三歲的教宗，在聖彼得廣場向信徒們進行每週一次奉告祈禱的佈告時，指出：「家庭本身掌握著社會的未來。」

　　羅馬天主教會和聯合國已經宣布一九九四年為國際家庭年，而且教會也草擬憲章，以促進父母與子女的權利。星期天在聖地的拿撒勒，正式宣布家庭年開始，並且舉行一場彌撒。根據聖經記載，此地是瑪麗和約瑟夫撫養耶穌基督的地方。

＊＊　pope〔pop〕n. 羅馬教皇　　　conception〔kən'sɛpʃən〕n. 懷孕
　　pontiff〔'pɑntɪf〕n.羅馬教皇　Angelus〔'ændʒələs〕n. 奉告祈禱
　　the faithful 忠實的信徒　　square〔skwɛr〕n. 廣場
　　Catholic〔'kæθəlɪk〕adj. 天主教的
　　declare〔dɪ'klɛr〕v. 宣布　　　***draw up*** 草擬
　　charter〔'tʃɑrtɚ〕n. 憲章　　　promote〔prə'mot〕v. 促進
　　inaugurate〔ɪn'ɔgjə,ret〕v. 開始　　mass〔mæs〕n. 彌撒
　　Nazareth〔'næzərəθ〕n. 拿撒勒　　***the Holy Land*** 聖地
　　Bible〔'baɪbl̩〕n. 聖經

Killing

Lions kill mango thief at zoo

Windhoek — Lions mauled to death a thief who broke into a zoo in Namibia to steal mangoes. The lions were let out of their enclosure at night to deter would-be thieves from crossing perimeter fences, said a keeper at Ekongoro zoo.

They were sitting next to the body of 20-year-old Lucas Tileni when officials opened the zoo on Sunday morning.

Tileni crossed a 3.5-meter (yard) double fence and a ditch to get into the zoo. Police said it was yet to be decided if any action should be taken against the lions or the zoo.

Bradley said he reared the lions from cubs and they were "as tame as pet dogs."

解答 ☞ p. 265

What is the purpose letting the lions out at night ?
(A) They are deterred from crossing the perimeter fence.
(B) They protect the master.
(C) They deter people from coming in to steal.
(D) They don't have to be enclosed at night.

動物園的獅子殺死芒果賊

溫德霍克電——在那米比亞，一位闖入動物園偷芒果的賊，被獅子傷害致死。艾康格洛動物園的看守員說，晚上他們會將獅子從圍欄中放出來，以防止打算偷東西的小偷跨越周圍的圍牆。

星期天早上職員打開動物園時，那些獅子正坐在二十歲的盧卡斯‧泰藍尼的屍體旁邊。

泰藍尼跨過3.5公尺（碼）的雙重圍牆，並越過排水溝，而潛入動物園。警方尚未決定是否要對那些獅子或動物園採取任何行動。

布雷德利指出，他把這些獅子從小養到大，牠們就像狗一樣溫馴。

** maul 〔mɔl〕 v. 打傷　　***break into*** 闖入
mango 〔'mæŋgo〕 n. 芒果　　enclosure 〔ɪn'kloʒɚ〕 n. 圍欄
deter 〔dɪ'tɝ〕 v. 防止　　would-be 〔'wʊd,bi〕 adj. 想要成為的
perimeter 〔pə'rɪmətɚ〕 n. 周圍　　fence 〔fɛns〕 n. 圍牆
ditch 〔dɪtʃ〕 n. 排水溝　　rear 〔rɪr〕 v. 飼養
cub 〔kʌb〕 n. 幼獸　　tame 〔tem〕 adj. 溫馴的

Trafficker   *Saturday Feb. 19*

Cocaine kingpin shot dead

Pablo Escobar, the world's most wanted cocaine trafficker, died in a rooftop shootout with Colombian police and soldiers on Dec. 2 after reigning for a decade over a ruthless global drug empire.

Colombian authorities said Escobar and a bodyguard fired at troopers who raided their three-story house. Police returned fire and killed them both as a barefoot Escobar tried to escape over a rooftop.

Escobar's death was not expected to seriously affect the daily flow of tons of cocaine from Colombia to the United States and other countries. His role in the drug trade declined drastically during 16 months as a fugitive.

But many Colombians breathed a sigh of relief after the killing of Escobar, who was accused of murdering hundreds of people during a reign marked by assassinations and car bombings that blew apart neighborhoods, shopping centers and a passenger airliner.

解答☞ p. 265

1. Why was Escobar " the world's most wanted " ?
   (A) Because he was ruthless.
   (B) Because he was in a shootout with Colombian police.
   (C) Because he was a cocaine addict.
   (D) Because he was a global cocaine dealer.

2. How was Escobar killed ?
   (A) He and a bodyguard opened fire and then were shot dead
       by police trying to escape over the roof.
   (B) The police raided Escobar's house and opened fire kill-
       ing him and a bodyguard.
   (C) Escobar, escaping over a rooftop, was shot dead by a
       bodyguard.
   (D) Escobar was shot dead because he returned to his house
       where the police were waiting for him on the rooftop.

3. What would the effect of Escobar's death on cocaine
   trafficking be ?
   (A) It would be great because of his drastic role in trafficking.
   (B) It would be small because his role in trafficking had
       decreased recently.
   (C) The flow of cocaine into the United States from
       Colombia would increase.
   (D) It would be small because the drug trade had already
       drastically declined.

4. Many Colombians were relieved because
   (A) the flow of cocaine would be slowed.
   (B) their country could get back to normal.
   (C) there would be fewer violent addicts.
   (D) Escobar was believed to be responsible for a lot of violence.

古柯鹼首腦被槍殺身亡

世界頭號古柯鹼毒梟厄斯可巴，於十二月二日在屋頂上與哥倫比亞軍警槍戰中喪生。十年來，他統治著一個冷酷殘忍的全球性毒品王國。

哥國當局表示，厄斯可巴和一名保鑣向突襲他們三層樓房子的警察開火。警方予以還擊，並在赤脚的厄斯可巴企圖爬過一個屋頂逃跑時，將他們雙雙擊斃。

每日自哥倫比亞向美國及其他國家流動的古柯鹼多達數噸，厄斯可巴之死對其影響不大。十六個月的逃亡生涯，使他的販毒事業大不如前。

但是，厄斯可巴死後，許多哥倫比亞人都鬆了一口氣，他被控殘殺數百條人命，由他操控的販毒集團以暗殺和在汽車中放炸彈著稱，炸彈曾炸毀鄰近住宅區、商場及一架客機。

＊＊ cocaine〔koˋken〕n. 古柯鹼　　kingpin〔ˊkɪŋ,pɪn〕n. 首腦
trafficker〔ˊtræfɪkɚ〕n. 走私者
shootout〔ˊʃut,aut〕n. 槍戰　　reign〔ren〕n. 統治
ruthless〔ˊruθlɪs〕adj. 冷酷的；殘忍的
bodyguard〔ˊbɑdɪ,gɑrd〕n. 保鑣　　trooper〔ˊtrupɚ〕n. 警察
raid〔red〕v. 襲擊　　decline〔dɪˋklaɪn〕v. 減弱
drastically〔ˊdræstɪkəlɪ〕adv. 徹底地
fugitive〔ˊfjudʒɚtɪv〕n. 逃亡者　　accuse〔əˋkjuz〕v. 控告
assassination〔ə,sæsnˋeʃən〕n. 暗殺
passenger〔ˊpæsndʒɚ〕n. 乘客
airliner〔ˊɛr,laɪnɚ〕n.（大型）客機

英文報紙必備社會用語

◇ L SD（lysergic acid dielhylamide）迷幻藥

◇ pot〔pɑt〕*n.*〔俚〕麻醉藥（尤指大麻）

◇ narcotic〔nɑr'kɑtɪk〕*n.* 麻醉藥

◇ amphetamine〔æm'fɛtə,min, -mɪn〕*n.* 安非他命

◇ addict〔'ædɪkt〕*n.*（麻醉毒品等的）上癮者

◇ guilty〔'gɪltɪ〕*adj.* 有罪的　　　fine〔faɪn〕*n.* 罰鍰

◇ investigate〔in'vɛstə,get〕*v.* 調查

◇ kidnap〔'kɪdnæp〕*v.* 綁架　　confess〔kən'fɛs〕*v.* 招認

◇ compensate〔'kɑmpən,set〕*v.* 賠償

◇ death penalty 死刑　　public prosecutor　檢察官

◇ jury〔'dʒʊrɪ〕*n.* 陪審團

◇ testimony〔'tɛstə,monɪ〕*n.*（法庭的）證言

◇ parole〔pə'rol〕*n.* 假釋　　victim〔'vɪktɪm〕*n.* 受害者

◇ bug〔bʌg〕*n.* 竊聽器　　　　judge〔dʒʌdʒ〕*n.* 法官

◇ suit〔sut, sjut〕*n.* 訴訟　　trial〔'traɪəl〕*n.* 審判

◇ amnesty〔'æm,nɛstɪ〕*n.* 特赦

◇ homicide〔'hɑmə,saɪd〕*n.* 殺人

◇ accuse〔ə'kjuz〕*v.* 控告　　verdict〔'vɝdɪkt〕*n.* 裁決

◇ fraud〔frɔd〕*n.* 詐欺　　raid〔red〕*n.* 搜捕

◇ criminal〔'krɪmən!〕*n.* 罪犯

◇ witness〔'wɪtnɪs〕*n.* 證人；目擊者

◇ civil court 民事法庭　　criminal court 刑事法庭

◇ uproar〔'ʌp,rɔr〕n. 騷動

◇ bribe〔braɪb〕n. 賄賂　v. 行賄

◇ national census 人口調查

◇ holocaust〔'hɑlə,kɔst〕n. 大屠殺

◇ employer〔ɪm'plɔɪɚ〕n. 雇主

◇ employee〔ɪm'plɔɪ·i, ,ɛmplɔɪ'i〕n. 受雇員工

◇ lockout〔'lɑk,aʊt〕n. 停工

◇ annuity〔ə'njuətɪ〕n. 養老金

◇ casualty〔'kæʒʊəltɪ〕n. 傷亡者

◇ indemnity〔ɪn'dɛmnətɪ〕n. 賠償金

◇ formality〔fɔr'mælətɪ〕n.（各種）手續

◇ illiteracy〔ɪ'lɪtərəsɪ〕n. 文盲

◇ refugee influx 難民流入　　output〔'aʊt,pʊt〕n. 產量

◇ national holiday 國定假日　　birth rate 出生率

◇ protest demonstration 示威遊行

◇ recruit〔rɪ'krut〕v. 招募

◇ promote〔prə'mot〕v. 晉級；促進

◇ anticipate〔æn'tɪsə,pet〕v. 預期

◇ manipulate〔mə'nɪpjə,let〕v. 操作；操縱

◇ intrude〔ɪn'trud〕v. 侵入；妨礙

◇ disengage〔,dɪsɪn'gedʒ〕v. 解脫

Accident　　　　　　　　　*Sunday July 17*

4 killed, 3 injured in highway pile-up

Compiled by
The China Post

Four people were killed and three others injured yesterday when 10 vehicles collided on a foggy section of the National Sun Yat-sen Freeway in central Taiwan, police said.

The Miaoli-Sanyi Section, where fogs have been blamed for many accidents in the past, has been the scene of crashes that claimed nine lives in the past two months, according to the police.

A truck loaded with wooden blocks triggered the accident at 4:30 a.m. yesterday when it rammed into the guard rail erected on the road divider on the freeway's foggy section after its left front tire burst.

Falling blocks from the crashed truck hit a private car running on the southbound freeway and driven by Lin Tseng-kuang.

Two other drivers and a passenger were also injured in the collision.

The pile-up disrupted highway traffic for more than three hours, said the police.

解答 ☞ p. 265

1. What has contributed to accidents in the Miaoli-Sanyi Section of the road?
   (A) vehicle overcrowding
   (B) excessive speed
   (C) poor weather conditions
   (D) driver fatigue

2. How did the accident start?
   (A) A truck hit a guard rail on the road divider.
   (B) A truck collided with a car with a burst tire.
   (C) A truck collided with a load of wooden blocks.
   (D) A guard rail hit a truck on the road in the fog.

3. What was the result of the crash?
   (A) The 10-car pileup caused further pileups on the highway.
   (B) The pile-up caused long delays for traffic.
   (C) Two drivers and a passenger were injured in another collision.
   (D) There were further disruptions in traffic because of the fog.

高速公路連環車禍，四死三傷

〔中國郵報〕警方指出，昨天在高速公路中部有霧路段，發生十輛車子追撞。車禍中四人死亡，三人受傷。

根據警方表示，在苗栗三義路段，起霧被斥為過去許多車禍發生的主因。據報導，在過去兩個月中，已有九人在此喪命。

昨天清晨四時廿五分，在此有霧路段，一輛滿載木頭的大貨車左前輪爆胎，之後，衝撞到中央分隔帶，而引起意外。

自貨車上掉落的木頭，擊中了當時在南下車道，由林增光所駕駛的私家轎車。

另有兩名駕駛及一名乘客在此追撞事件中受傷。

警方指出，這起連環車禍使高速公路交通受阻長達三個多小時。

**　injure 〔ˈɪndʒɚ〕 v. 受傷　　pile-up 〔ˈpaɪlˌʌp〕 n. 連環車禍
　vehicle 〔ˈviɪkl̩〕 n. 車輛　　collide 〔kəˈlaɪd〕 v. 互撞
　crash 〔kræʃ〕 v. 撞碎　　trigger 〔ˈtrɪɡɚ〕 v. 引起
　ram into 撞入　　southbound 〔ˈsaʊθˌbaʊnd〕 adj. 往南的

Japanese trends

Wednesday Jan. 5

1 out of 4 will be elderly by 2025

Reuter

Tokyo, Jan. 4—Japan will have the oldest society of all the world's top economic powers by the year 2025, according to a government report issued on Tuesday.

It said 25.8 percent of the population would be aged 65 or over. On a comparative scale using United Nations statistics, Germany would rank second with 23 percent, followed by the United States with 20 percent and Britain 19 percent.

Japan already ranks top in terms of life expectancy, the report said, with an average life span for women of 82 years and 76 years for men.

Public concern is growing about how the social welfare system will cope, according to the study.

In a recent survey of 2,300 people, 70 percent said they feared the government would not be able to provide adequate pensions or enough nursing homes in the next century.

The report said 89 percent of those polled were concerned they would not be able to take care of themselves or their spouses in their old age. Many feared being bed-ridden.

解答☞ p. 265

1. By the year 2025, Japan
   (A) will have a majority of old citizens.
   (B) will have more rich people than any other economic power.
   (C) will have a larger percentage of old people than any other economic power.
   (D) will have been an economic power for longer than any other nation.

2. According to the report,
   (A) the quality of life is better in Japan than in the other countries.
   (B) people in Japan generally live longer than in the other countries.
   (C) Japanese men and women know what to expect from life.
   (D) On average women live longer than men.

3. According to a survey, a majority feared
   (A) the government would go bankrupt.
   (B) they would lose their pension.
   (C) there wouldn't be enough nurses to visit homes.
   (D) there would be insufficient funds for pension and a shortage of nursing homes.

4. 89% of those polled
   (A) were afraid that they would be left on their own.
   (B) were afraid of being confined to bed and unable to look after themselves or their spouses.
   (C) were afraid that their spouse would die.
   (D) were afraid there wouldn't be any nurses so they couldn't leave their beds.

2025年之前將有四分之一的人口是老人

〔路透社〕東京，一月四日電──根據星期二官方的報告指出，西元2025年之前，日本將是經濟大國中，最高齡化的社會。

報告指出，百分之二十五點八的人口將達到六十五歲或超過六十五歲。以美國的統計方式來作比較等級，德國的百分之二十三排第二，接下來是百分之二十的美國，以及百分之十九的英國。

報告並指出，日本的平均壽命已到世界之冠，女人壽命平均八十二歲，男人七十二歲。

根據此項研究，如何讓社會福利體系跟進的公共事業正在發展中。

最近在一個對兩千三百人做的調查當中，有百分之七十的人表示，他們擔心政府將無法在下一個世紀提供充裕的養老金，或足夠的養老院。

報告中並指出百分之八十九的受訪者擔心，當他們年老的時候，無法照顧自己或配偶，許多人還擔心會臥病不起。

** issue 〔ˈɪʃjʊ〕 v. 公布　comparative 〔kəmˈpærətɪv〕 adj. 比較的
scale 〔skel〕 n. 等級　statistics 〔stəˈtɪstɪks〕 n. 統計
in terms of ~ 從~觀點　*life expectancy* 平均壽命
span 〔spæn〕 n. 期間　adequate 〔ˈædəkwɪt〕 adj. 充分的
pension 〔ˈpɛnʃən〕 n. 養老金　spouse 〔spaʊz〕 n. 配偶
bedridden 〔ˈbɛd͵rɪdn̩〕 adj. 臥病不起

Surrogacy

Saturday Nov. 16

'Womb-for-rent' ad on highway billboard

Associated Press

Houston, Nov. 14 — Above the highway buzz of Houston's traffic reads this billboard:

"Womb for Rent! Educated, Healthy, Loving, Surrogate Mother Available."

The woman, who wants to remain anonymous, said she hopes some prospective parents will call her lawyer so she can help an infertile couple and also meet some of her own goals, such as using part of her fee to complete a doctorate.

"They say that if a woman is motivated by money, then she should not be considered···but why else would a woman become pregnant if it weren't to satisfy a goal, be it financial or another goal?" she said.

The woman said she had been considering surrogacy for the last five years. The woman is seeking more than the average US $10,000 that usually goes to surrogates because of her healthy status and educational background. She has a master's degree in biology.

" I talked it over with my husband and he said, ' It's your body and your womb and you can do anything you want to,'" she said.

解答 ☞ p. 265

1. What is the woman advertising to do?
   (A) Looking for a father for her baby.
   (B) Looking to rent a womb.
   (C) Trying to help an infertile couple have a child.
   (D) Trying to adopt some children.

2. What price is the woman seeking for her surrogacy?
   (A) $10,000.
   (B) $10,000 or the nearest offer.
   (C) More than the average $10,000 because of her qualifications.
   (D) The price of her doctorate.

3. What is her husband's attitude to this?
   (A) He is against it.
   (B) He wanted her to do it.
   (C) He thinks it should be her decision.
   (D) He can't decide.

公路看板上的「子宮出租」廣告

〔美聯社〕休士頓，十一月十四日——在休士頓交通繁忙的公路上，有個廣告看板上面這麼寫著：

「子宮出租！提供受過教育、健康又仁慈的代理孕母。」

這名不願透露姓名的女人說，她希望會有一些求子心切的夫妻，打電話給她的律師。如此一來，不但可以幫助不孕的夫妻，也可達成自己的一些目標，例如，用部分的收費來完成博士學位。

她說：「有人說，如果女人的動機是錢，那麼她就不該予以考慮…但是，如果不是爲了達成某個目標，不論這是財務上或其他的目標，女人爲何要懷孕呢？」

這名女子表示，她考慮做代理孕母了。一般借腹生子平均費用爲一萬美元，但她因爲自己的健康狀況和教育背景，而索價更多。她擁有生物學碩士的學位。

她表示：「我和我先生談過，他說：『這是你的身體，你的子宮，你可以做任何想做的事。』」

✻✻ womb〔wum〕*n.* 子宮　　billboard〔'bɪl,bord〕*n.* 廣告看板
buzz〔bʌz〕*n.* 匆忙地四處活動　　surrogate〔'sɝɪgɪt〕*n.* 代理者
anonymous〔ə'nɑnəməs〕*adj.* 不具名的
prospective〔prə'spɛktɪv〕*adj.* 預期的
motivate〔'motə,vet〕*v.* 引起動機
pregnant〔'prɛgnənt〕*adj.* 懷孕的　　surrogacy〔'sɝə,gesɪ〕*n.* 借腹生子
negotiable〔nɪ'goʃəbl̩〕*adj.* 可磋商的
supportive〔sə'portɪv〕*adj.* 支持的

Britain

Tuesday Aug. 30

Royalty is Britain's image

Market research among holidaymakers in Britain and attitude surveys show royalty, heritage and pageantry rank as one of the UK's greatest attractions.

Buckingham Palace is named more often than any other London attraction by overseas visitors asked to say which places they had planned to visit before leaving their own country.

Nearly one in three people questioned for the survey done in 1992 among overseas visitors in the capital mentioned Buckingham Palace, and 30 percent named the Tower of London.

One in five long-haul visitors pick London because of its history and pageantry-in which royalty past and present obviously plays a leading role. In Britain as a whole, visiting heritage sites is the single most popular pastime among overseas holidaymakers.

Almost half the overseas summer holidaymakers in London have plans to watch the Changing of the Guard at Buckingham Palace. Among first-time visitors, the figure is more than 60 percent.

解答 ☞ p. 265

■ What does the survey say attracts visitors to Britain?
(A) cuisine
(B) scenery
(C) culture and traditions
(D) holiday resorts

皇室是英國的典型代表

一項針對英國渡假之旅客的市場研究和態度調查顯示，英國最吸引人之處，以皇室、文化遺產和景物壯觀名列前茅。

當國外旅客動身離開之前，被問及計劃要去的地方，他們大多回答白金漢宮，而不是倫敦其他旅遊勝地。

在針對一九九二年來訪首府的國外旅客的調查中，每三人就有一人提及白金漢宮，而有百分之三十的受訪者提及倫敦塔。

有五分之一做長途旅行的人，因歷史及壯觀因素而選擇倫敦。在倫敦，皇室在過去及現在很顯然的扮演了主角。就整體來說，拜訪英國境內的文化古蹟，是唯一最受國外遊客歡迎的消遣。

夏日遊訪倫敦的旅客中，幾乎有一半的人計劃去看白金漢宮侍衞的交接。在第一次來訪的旅客中，數據更超過了百分之六十。

** royalty〔ˈrɔɪəltɪ〕n. 皇室　　survey〔ˈsɜve〕n. 調查
heritage〔ˈhɛrətɪdʒ〕n.（文化）遺產
pageantry〔ˈpædʒəntrɪ〕n. 壯觀
Buckingham Palace 白金漢宮　　the Tower of London 倫敦塔
long-haul〔ˈlɔŋˈhɔl〕adj. 長距離的　*play a ~ role* 扮演～的角色
as a whole 整體而言　　site〔saɪt〕n. 地點
guard〔gɑrd〕n. 衞兵

Travel

Sunday Oct. 12

S.Africa targets Asian tourists

By Christopher Bodeen
Special to The China Post

Seeking to overcome a reputation for racial antipathy and political violence, South Africa is aggressively promoting tourism.

In doing so it is turning much of its attention to Asia. Arrivals from Asia have rivaled those from North America over the last two years, totaling almost 5,000 in 1992 and expected to exceed that figure this year.

With multi-party elections scheduled for next April, South African tourism officials are hoping to reassure potential visitors that the country's turbulent period is drawing to a close. Today they are promoting their country as a " new safe destination, an exciting destination, an important destination to discover. "

解答 ☞ p. 265

1. What is the reputation South Africa has to overcome?
   (A) a reputation for racial and political conflict
   (B) a reputation for racial and political diversity
   (C) a reputation for aggressive tourism
   (D) a poor reputation for tourist facilities

2. Why is South Africa turning its attention to Asia?
   (A) It is trying to overcome its reputation for racial antipathy.
   (B) North American tourists have declined in numbers.
   (C) Asian countries are now rivaling North America in investment and visits.
   (D) Because it has close relations with Taiwan.

3. What is the hope for effect of the scheduled elections?
   (A) A new government will take charge and change policies.
   (B) New laws will be enacted promting tourism.
   (C) The new government will emphasize law and order.
   (D) The country's current difficult situation will end.

文中提及的多黨選舉，是指一九九四年四月間的
總統大選，其標榜的最大特色是不分種族、平等
的選舉。結果由非洲民族黨（ANC）領袖曼德拉
獲勝，成為南非首任黑人總統。曼德拉總統上任
後，雖然百廢待舉，但他以高昂的鬥志，欲實現
民族平等，率南非加入非洲團結組織，籲族裔和
睦相處，並撥款濟助貧困黑人。

南非瞄準亞洲觀光客

〔中國郵報〕爲了除去種族歧視和政治暴動的惡名，南非政府正積極地推廣觀光事業。

爲了擴展觀光，南非將注意力轉向亞洲地區。在過去兩年中，從亞洲來的觀光客已能和北美來的媲美，一九九二年其旅遊人數幾近五千人次，而今年可望超出這個數字。

由於排定明年四月爲多黨選舉，南非政府負責觀光事業的官員，希望這些極有潛力的觀光客放心，南非的動亂即將告一段落。目前他們正努力將南非提昇爲「嶄新、安全、刺激而重要的旅遊地點，值得人們去發現。」

** target 〔'tɑrgɪt〕 n. 對象；目標　　tourist 〔'tʊrɪst〕 n. 觀光客
reputation 〔ˌrɛpjə'teʃən〕 n.名聲　　racial 〔'reʃəl〕 adj. 種族的
antipathy 〔æn'tɪpəθɪ〕 n. 反感；不相容
violence 〔'vaɪələns〕 n. 暴力
aggressively 〔ə'grɛsɪvlɪ〕 adv. 積極的
promote 〔prə'mot〕 v. 提昇　　tourism 〔'tʊrɪzm〕 n. 觀光事業
rival 〔'raɪvl〕 v. 競爭　　exceed 〔ɪk'sid〕 v. 超越
multi-party 〔ˌmʌltɪ'pɑrtɪ〕 adj. 多黨的
schedule 〔'skɛdʒʊl〕 v.預定　　potential 〔pə'tɛnʃəl〕 adj. 有潛力的
turbulent 〔'tɝbjələnt〕 adj. 動亂的
destination 〔ˌdɛstə'neʃən〕 n. (旅行的)目的地

英文報紙必備文化用語

◇ classical music 古典樂　　symphony〔'sɪmfənɪ〕n. 交響樂
◇ rock and roll（rock n' roll）搖滾樂
◇ folk song 民歌　　jazz music 爵士樂
◇ pop music 流行音樂　　staff〔stæf〕n. 五線譜
◇ orchestra〔'ɔrkɪstrə〕n. 管弦樂團
◇ choir〔kwaɪr〕n. 合唱團
◇ violin〔,vaɪə'lɪn〕n. 小提琴

◇ cello〔'tʃɛlo〕n. 大提琴　　harp〔hɑrp〕n. 豎琴
◇ harmonica〔hɑr'mɑnɪkə〕n. 口琴
◇ trumpet〔'trʌmpɪt〕n. 喇叭
◇ French horn 法國號
◇ sculpture〔'skʌlptʃɚ〕n. 雕刻
◇ calligraphy〔kə'lɪɡrəfɪ〕n. 書法
◇ illustration〔ɪ,lʌs'treʃən〕n. 插圖
◇ print〔prɪnt〕n. 版畫　　canvas〔'kænvəs〕n. 油畫

◇ easel〔'izl̩〕n. 畫架
◇ sketch〔skɛtʃ〕n. 寫生；素描
◇ spoken drama 話劇　　opera〔'ɑpərə〕n. 歌劇
◇ musical drama 歌舞劇　　classical play 古典戲劇
◇ curtain〔'kɝtɪn〕n. 幕　　lines〔laɪnz〕n. 台詞
◇ script〔skrɪpt〕n. 劇本

◇ director〔də'rɛktɚ〕n. 導演

◇ conductor〔kən'dʌktɚ〕n. 指揮

◇ playwright〔'ple,raɪt〕; dramatist〔'dræmətɪst〕n. 劇作家

◇ auditorium〔,ɔdə'torɪəm〕n. 聽衆席；大禮堂

◇ poem〔'po·ɪm〕n. 詩   ode〔od〕n. 賦；抒情詩

◇ lyric〔'lɪrɪk〕n. 抒情詩   sonnet〔'sɑnɪt〕n. 十四行詩

◇ the classics 古典文學   contemporary literature 當代文學

◇ biographical literature 傳記文學

◇ love story 愛情小說

◇ romance〔ro'mæns〕n. 冒險故事；愛情小說

◇ whodunit〔hu'dʌnɪt〕n. 偵探小說（= detective story）

◇ knight-errant novel 武俠小說   science fiction 科幻小說

◇ intellectual property rights 智慧財產權

◇ gallery〔'gælərɪ〕n.；arts museum 美術館

◇ museum〔mju'zɪəm〕n. 博物館

◇ observatory〔əb'zɝvə,torɪ〕n. 天文台

◇ opera house 歌劇院   music hall 音樂廳

◇ castle〔'kæsl̩〕n. 城堡   palace〔'pælɪs〕n. 宮殿

◇ cathedral〔kə'θidrəl〕n. 大教堂

◇ temple〔'tɛmpl̩〕n. 寺廟   mosque〔mɑsk〕n. 清眞寺

◇ pyramid〔'pɪrəmɪd〕n. 金字塔

◇ shrine〔ʃraɪn〕n. 聖殿；祠堂

◇ antique〔æn'tik〕n. 古董

Job market

About 6 million defer work

About six million people, or more than 40 percent of the population who are over 15 years old, did not join the work force in 1992, according to figures released yesterday by the Directorate-General of Budget, Accounting and Statistics.

Of the six million people, 2.6 million, or 43 percent, said they had to attend to their homes while 1.8 million, or 29 percent, were studying or preparing to continue their studies.

In another report, the DGBAS noted that the tax burden on individuals had risen by an average of 12 percent a year between 1986 and 1992.

In 1986, the per capita tax burden was $20,864. In 1992, it had increased to $46,926.

The tax revenues in Taiwan had been about 20 percent of the gross national product in recent years, the agency said, which were slightly lower than those in the US, Japan and Switzerland.

解答☞ p.265

1. Why did more than 40 percent of the workforce not work ?
   (A) Lack of suitable employment opportunities to attend.
   (B) They were working at home.
   (C) They were studying at home.
   (D) They were doing housework or studying.

2. What happened to the tax rate on individuals ?
   (A) It increased by 12 percent between 1986 and 1992.
   (B) It increased annually by 12 percent between 1986 and 1992.
   (C) It decreased annually by 12 percent between 1986 and 1992.
   (D) It approximately increased as a percentage between 1986 and 1992.

3. "Per capita" means :
   (A) total   (B) divided up
   (C) each person   (D) tax rate

4. What was the tax revenue situation in the last few years ?
   (A) It was about 20 percent lower than before.
   (B) Japan, Switzerland and the U.S.'s revenues were slightly lower.
   (C) It was about 20 percent of national income, lower than in some rich countries.
   (D) It had produced 20 percent of gross product, more than in 1986.

約六百萬人延緩加入工作行列

預算會統處處長指出，一九九二年，大約六百萬人，也就是超過百分之四十的十五歲以上的人口沒有加入工作行列。

六百萬人之中，有兩百六十萬人，也就是百分之四十三的人口，說他們必須照顧家庭，而一百八十萬的人，也就是百分之二十九的人口正在讀書，或準備繼續升學。

在另一篇報告中，預算會統處處長亦注意到在一九八六年到一九九二年之間，每人負擔的稅額平均每年提高百分之十二。

在一九八六年，個人所負擔的稅額是兩萬零八百六十四美元，而在一九九二年，已增加到四萬六千九百二十六元。

該機關並指出，近幾年來，台灣的稅收大約佔國家總生產的百分之二十，比美國、日本和瑞士稍低。

** defer〔dɪˈfɝ〕v. 延緩　　release〔rɪˈlis〕v. 解脫；發表
directorate〔dəˈrɛktərɪt〕n. 主管職位
budget〔ˈbʌdʒɪt〕n. 預算　　accounting〔əˈkaʊntɪŋ〕n. 會計
statistics〔stəˈtɪstɪks〕n. 統計　　burden〔ˈbɝdn̩〕n. 負擔
individual〔ˌɪndəˈvɪdʒʊəl〕n. 個人　　*per capita* 每人的
revenue〔ˈrɛvəˌnju〕n. 稅收　　gross〔gros〕adj. 總計的
agency〔ˈedʒənsɪ〕n. 政府機關

England   *Wednesday Dec. 27*

Charles and Diana put on family faces

Reuter

London, Dec. 25 — Prince Charles and his estranged wife Princess Diana made a show of Christmas family unity on Saturday, striding to church with their two sons.

The heir to the throne and Diana joined most of the rest of Britain's royal family at Queen Elizabeth's Sandringham estate in the eastern English county of Norfolk. All strolled past waiting crowds to the annual royal Christmas church service.

Charles walked with their oldest son, Prince William, while Diana followed a short distance behind with the younger Prince Harry.

Diana left soon after the service to join her brother, the Earl Spencer, at their family estate in central England,

Missing from the annual royal Christmas outing was the Duchess of York, the former Sarah Ferguson, who is the estranged wife of Andrew the Duke of York. She was reported by seasoned royal watchers to be staying in a small house on the Sandringham estate with her two children, Beatrice and Eugenie.

解答☞ p. 265

1. Prince Charles went with Princess Diana and their sons to church because :
   (A) it was Christmas when many families go to church.
   (B) it would be strange for them not to go together.
   (C) they always go to church as a family.
   (D) they wanted to show unity at Christmas despite family problems.

2. After the service, Prince Charles and Princess Diana
   (A) separated and went to different estates.
   (B) joined the Queen at her Sandringham estate.
   (C) strolled past crowds of people waiting to see them.
   (D) took their sons, Prince William and Prince Harry for a walk.

3. Which sentence best describes the Duchess of York's situation ? She:
   (A) used to be called Sarah Ferguson.
   (B) is estranged from her husband and did not attend the service.
   (C) could not attend the service because she had to look after her children.
   (D) lives on the Queen's estate, but not in the same house.

查理與戴安娜重拾天倫面具

〔路透社〕倫敦，十二月二十五日電──查理王子偕其感情失和的妻子戴安娜王妃，在星期六一同與他們兩個兒子步入教堂時，顯現出一幅家庭和諧的景象。

這位王室繼承人和戴安娜前往伊莉莎白女皇在英國東部諾福克郡的聖瑞罕邸宅，與多位其他的英國皇室家族會面。一行人行經等候的群眾後，便開始一年一度的聖誕禮拜。

查理和大兒子威廉王子走在一起，而戴安娜則與小兒子哈利王子委隨在後。

戴安娜在禮拜之後，便立刻前往她們家族位於英格蘭中部的邸宅，與哥哥史賓塞伯爵會面。

約克公爵夫人並沒有出席這次一年一度的聖誕出遊，她是莎拉‧弗格森，也就是和約克公爵安德魯感情失和的妻子。據有經驗的皇室觀察者報導，她與她的兩個孩子碧翠絲和尤金妮住在聖瑞罕的一間小屋中。

** ***put on*** 戴上　　estranged 〔ə'strendʒd〕 *adj.* 疏離的；不和的
unity 〔'junətɪ〕 *n.* 統一；合諧　　stride 〔straɪd〕 *v.* 前進
heir 〔ɛr〕 *n.* 繼承人　throne 〔θron〕 *n.* 王位
royal 〔'rɔɪər〕 *adj.* 王室的　　estate 〔ə'stet〕 *n.* 財產；土地
annual 〔'ænjuəl〕 *adj.* 一年一度的　　earl 〔ɝl〕 *n.* 伯爵
outing 〔'autɪŋ〕 *n.* 郊遊　　duchess 〔'dʌtʃɪs〕 *n.* 女公爵
duke 〔djuk〕 *n.* 公爵　　seasoned 〔'siznd〕 *adj.* 有經驗的

Three youths shot by officer

Three youths were in stable condition yesterday after they were shot by a police officer when they tried to speed away from a roadside check.

Each boy was hit by at least one bullet, police said.

The youths' parents accused the officer, who fired 12 rounds, of over-reacting. But the officer claimed he acted in self-defense, saying he was dragged about 300 meters down the street after one of the youths grabbed him from inside the car and the driver took off.

The driver, who didn't have a license, was taking two of his friends out for a night drive.

解答 ☞ p.265

1. The three youths were shot
    (A) as they were speeding.
    (B) because they didn't have a license.
    (C) when they fled the check-point.
    (D) after they were checked.

2. Why did the parents accuse the officer of overreacting?
    (A) Because the victims were only youths.
    (B) Because he fired so many rounds.
    (C) Because each of the youths was hit by at least one bullet.
    (D) Because the car was only speeding.

3. Why did the police officer claim it was in self-defense?
    (A) Because the youths would have killed him.
    (B) Because unlicensed youths are dangerous.
    (C) Because the youths dragged him down the street.
    (D) Because the youths weren't killed.

Focus

●法律相關字彙

acquittal〔ə'kwɪtl〕n. 不起訴

alibi〔'ælə,baɪ〕n.案發時,被告不在場的答辯

infancy〔'ɪnfənsɪ〕n. 未成年

turf〔tɝf〕n. 都市中地痞流氓的勢力範圍

三名年輕人被警官射傷

三位年輕人企圖加速衝過路邊臨檢站時，被一名警察開槍射傷，目前傷勢已穩定下來。

警方表示，每位男孩至少身中一發子彈。

這名警官共開了十二槍，而這三名年輕人的父母要控告他反應過度，執法不當。但這名警官聲稱他是基於自衛，他表示，當時，他被這三名年輕人自車中拉出，而後，駕駛者開動車子，並將他沿著街道拖了三百多公尺。

這位無照駕駛的年輕人，當時正載著另兩名男孩出外夜遊。

** stable〔'stebl̩〕*adj.* 穩定的
　　bullet〔'bʊlɪt〕*n.* 子彈
　　accuse〔ə'kjuz〕*v.* 控告
　　overreact〔,ovərɪ'ækt〕*v.* 反應過度
　　self-defense〔,sɛlfdɪ'fɛns〕*n.* 自衛
　　drag〔dræg〕*v.* 拖；拉
　　grab〔græb〕*v.* 抓住　　***take off*** 動身
　　license〔'laɪsn̩s〕*n.* 執照

Espionage   *Thursday Mar. 3*

Male spy appears in women's clothes

In a new twist to a recent flurry of espionage cases, a German male postal worker appeared in court on spying charges—dressed as a woman.

A Cologne newspaper said Ruediger H, 64, whose full name was withheld, wore a wig and earrings and carried a handbag as he faced charges of spying for East Germany.

He is accused of opening 2,100 items of mail intended for the German armed forces or military intelligence and passing information from the naval harbor at Kiel to East Berlin. But he said there was no connection between his espionage activities and his transvestism.

解答 ☞ p. 265

◼ What did the man say about his transvestism?

(A) He appears in women's clothes for espionage.

(B) There was no connection between his espionage activities and his guise.

(C) He disguised himself for the convenience of opening 2,100 items of mail.

(D) He dressed as a woman because he was a postal worker.

男扮女裝的德國間諜

最近一連串的德國間諜案中，又有了意外的發展——一名德國郵局男性員工因涉嫌從事間諜活動而出庭應訊——打扮成女人的樣子。

科隆市一家報紙指出，這名未公佈全名的六十四歲男子魯迪傑，被控爲東德從事間諜活動，他戴著一頂假髮和耳環，還拿著一只手提袋。

他被控擅自打開送往德國軍隊或軍事情報局的二千一百個郵件，並將資料由位於凱爾的海軍軍港送至東柏林。但他說他從事間諜活動與男扮女裝之事並無關聯。

** spy〔spaɪ〕n. 間諜　　　　twist〔twɪst〕n. 意外的發展
flurry〔'flɝɪ〕n. 混亂　　espionage〔'ɛspɪə,nɑʒ〕n. 間諜行爲
withhold〔wɪð'hold, wɪθ-〕v. 保留　　　wig〔wɪg〕n. 假髮
accuse〔ə'kjuz〕v. 控告
intelligence〔ɪn'tɛlədʒəns〕n. 情報
naval〔'nevl̩〕adj. 海軍的　　　harbor〔'hɑrbɚ〕n. 海港
East Berlin 東柏林
transvestism〔træns'vɛstɪzm̩, trænz-〕n. 易裝之癖好

Esthetics

Thursday May 12

East-West study: Human beauty is universal

*By **Maggie Fox***
Reuter

London — People all over the world generally agree on what makes a human face beautiful, British and Japanese psychologists reported recently.

Sexless, unbiased computers were used to reach a conclusion. Beautiful women have high cheekbones and large eyes. Attractive men have strong chins.

It's the same everywhere, said a report in the science journal *Nature*.

The effect worked across cultures. "Japanese and Caucasian observers showed the same direction of preferences for the same facial composites, suggesting that esthetic judgments of face shape are similar across different cultural backgrounds."

解答 ☞ p. 265

1. What did the British/Japanese study conclude?

    (A) Beauty is only skin-deep.

    (B) Beauty is in the eye of the beholder.

    (C) Beauty has common human traits.

    (D) Beauty is a cultural phenomenon.

2. What was the purpose of the computers?

    (A) to be biased

    (B) to be subjective

    (C) to be neutral

    (D) to be selective

3. What does the study suggest about male and female beauty?

    (A) Beauty in men and women follows the same traits.

    (B) Men and women have different opinions as to beauty.

    (C) Beauty is widespread around the world.

    (D) Beauty in men and women is emphasized in different traits.

審美標準全球公認

〔路透社〕倫敦電——英國和日本的心理學家最近指出，全世界各地的人大致公認什麼樣的臉孔是最漂亮的。

無性別，無偏見的電腦被用來做結論分析。結果指出，美麗的女人有高聳的顴骨和大眼睛，而迷人的男性則有結實的下顎。

科學期刊「自然」中的一篇報導指出，世界各地的審美標準大致如此。

這項結果在各種不同的文化都通用。「日本人和白種人的觀察家對於上述的五官組合，同樣地都顯出偏好。這也說明了不同文化背景的人，對臉部輪廓的審美觀卻很類似。」

**　universal〔͵junəˋvɝsl〕adj. 共同的
　　British〔ˋbrɪtɪʃ〕adj. 英國的
　　Japanese〔͵dʒæpəˋniz〕adj. 日本的
　　psychologist〔saɪˋkɑlədʒɪst〕n. 心理學家
　　sexless〔ˋsɛkslɪs〕adj. 無性別的
　　unbiased〔ʌnˋbaɪəst〕adj. 無偏見的
　　cheekbone〔ˋtʃik͵bon〕n. 顴骨
　　chin〔tʃɪn〕n. 下顎　　　journal〔ˋdʒɝnḷ〕n. 期刊
　　Caucasian〔kɔˋkeʃən〕adj. 白種人的
　　observer〔əbˋzɝvɚ〕n. 觀察者
　　preference〔ˋprɛfərəns〕n. 偏愛
　　composite〔kəmˋpɑzɪt〕n. 組成；合成物
　　esthetic〔ɛsˋθɛtɪk〕adj. 美學的

Poll   *Monday May 2*

Macau likes ROC better than HK does

By Ta Yu-shan
The China Post

An opinion poll shows that residents in Macau have a better impression of Taiwan than Hong Kong residents do, but, at the same time they expect more from the ROC government.

Hong Kong, a British colony, will revert to mainland Chinese rule in 1997, while Macau, a Portuguese colony, will be taken over by the mainland in 1999.

According to the poll, more than 50 percent of the respondents in Macau have a better impres-  sion of Taiwan than Hong Kong residents, while 26.3 percent of Macau's residents have considered immigrating to Taiwan before the 1999 takeover.

Some 89 percent support Taiwan maintaining its Macau offices after 1999.

解答 ☞ p.265

1. What is the attitude of the residents of Macau?
   (A) They prefer Macau and Hong Kong to Taiwan.
   (B) They like Taiwan, but are wary of the ROC government.
   (C) They like Hong Kong more than Taiwan.
   (D) They have a better impression of Taiwan and its government than Hong Kongers.

2. What is the situation regarding the two colonies?
   (A) Hong Kong and Macau will revert to China in 1997, and 1999 respectively.
   (B) Macau will revert to China prior to Hong Kong in 1997.
   (C) Hong Kong and Macau will be colonies of Mainland China.
   (D) Both will retain ROC offices.

3. What does the opinion poll claim?
   (A) 50% more Macau residents would rather live in Taiwan than Hong Kong.
   (B) About one in four Macau residents has considered immigration to Taiwan.
   (C) 89% of Macau residents support the ROC government.
   (D) Hong Kong has a poor image of Taiwan.

澳門對台灣印象良好

〔中國郵報〕根據一項民意調查顯示，澳門居民對台灣的印象，比香港居民好。但同時，他們對於中華民國政府的期望較高。

香港是英國殖民地，將於一九九七年歸還大陸管轄，而澳門是葡萄牙殖民地，也將於一九九九年交還中共。

根據這項民調，有百分之五十以上的澳門受訪者對台灣的印象，比香港人對台灣的印象好。而且，有百分之二十六點三的澳門居民考慮在九九大限前移民台灣。

百分之八十九的澳門人支持台灣於一九九九年後，仍保留駐澳門辦事處。

** Macau〔məˈkɑʊ〕*n.* 澳門

　　resident〔ˈrɛzədənt〕*n.* 居民

　　colony〔ˈkɑlənɪ〕*n.* 殖民地

　　revert〔rɪˈvɝt〕*v.* 歸還

　　Portuguese〔ˈpɔrtʃəˌgiz〕*adj.* 葡萄牙的

　　take over 接收

　　respondent〔rɪˈspɑndənt〕*n.* 受訪者

　　immigrate〔ˈɪməˌgret〕*v.* 移民（移入）

　　takeover〔ˈtekˌovɚ〕*n.* 接收

　　maintain〔menˈtenˌmən-〕*v.* 維持

Part 3

Politics & Military 政治軍事

Army

Lee inspects new copters from U.S.

Compiled by The China Post

The ROC Army demonstrated its recently enhanced aerial attack and surveillance capabilities by showing 12 U.S.-made attack and scout helicopters at an army base yesterday.

ROC President Lee Teng-hui inspected the eight AH-1W Cobra attack gunships and four OH-58D Kiowa warrior scout helicopters, which were delivered last month, at Kwei-jen Army Base in southern Taiwan yesterday.

The helicopters shown yesterday are part of a US$1.2 billion (NT$30 billion) arms deal to purchase 42 Cobras and 26 Kiowas from the U.S.

Lee expressed confidence in the new helicopters. "With these superior helicopters, our army's warfare capability is significantly boosted," he added.

The OH-58D was developed in the early 1980s to provide the U.S. Army with reconnaissance helicopters capable of intelligence gathering, surveillance, as well as supporting attack helicopter missions and directing artillery fire.

解答 ☞ p.265

1. The ROC Army recently improved its aerial attack capabilities by
   (A) increased training of troops.
   (B) taking delivery of 12 U.S.-made helicopters.
   (C) buying attack ships from the U.S.
   (D) purchasing ammunition from the U.S.

2. The Taiwan government has made a deal with the U.S. to
   (A) design and manufacture helicopters in Taiwan.
   (B) sell the U.S. $1.2 billion in arms.
   (C) purchase US$30 billion in arms.
   (D) buy 42 Cobra and 26 Kiowa helicopters.

3. The OH-58D helicopter is designed to
   (A) gather intelligence and support attack missions.
   (B) tolerate damage by weapons up to 23mm.
   (C) transport President Lee Teng-hui on official missions.
   (D) take tourists for a ride when they visit Kwei-jen Army base.

李總統視察向美新購之直昇機

〔中國郵報〕我國軍昨日在一陸軍基地展示十二架美製攻擊、及偵察直昇機，以證明陸軍日益強大的空中攻擊及警戒能力。

李登輝總統昨日親臨南台灣歸仁陸軍基地，視察上個月運到的八架AH-1W超級眼鏡蛇武裝攻擊直昇機，及四架OH-58D凱歐瓦戰士偵察直昇機。

昨日展示的直昇機，是我與美武器採購協定的一部分，總金額十二億美元（台幣三百億元），共採購攻擊直昇機四十二架，及偵察直昇機二十六架。

李總統對新購直昇機深具信心，並說：「有了這些優異的直昇機後，我陸軍戰力必大幅提昇。」

OH-58D是在1980年代被發展出來，供美國陸軍使用的偵察直昇機，不但能擔任攻擊直昇機的任務和提供直接大砲火力攻擊，也具有蒐集情報和偵察的功能。

** inspect〔ɪnˈspɛkt〕*v.* 視察   copter〔ˈkɑptə〕*n.* 直昇機
demonstrate〔ˈdɛmənˌstret〕*v.* 展示
aerial〔ˈɛrɪəl〕*adj.* 空中的
surveillance〔səˈveləns〕*n.* 監視   scout〔skaʊt〕*n.* 偵察機（艦）
helicopter〔ˈhɛlɪˌkɑptə, ˈhi-〕*n.* 直昇機
cobra〔ˈkobrə〕*n.* 眼鏡蛇   warrior〔ˈwɔrɪɚ, ˈwɑr-〕*n.* 戰士
purchase〔ˈpɝtʃəs〕*v.* 購買   boost〔bust〕*v.* 增加
reconnaissance〔rɪˈkɑnəsəns〕*n.* 偵察
artillery〔arˈtɪlərɪ〕*n.* 大砲

Puerto Rico

Monday Dec. 15

Puerto Rican voters reject independence

SAN JUAN, Puerto Rico — Rejecting the strongest campaign this century for full union with the United States, Puerto Rico voted to remain a US commonwealth rather than become the 51st American state.

Yesterday's vote hinged on ethnic pride and economics and was the first ballot in 26 years on Puerto Rico's political future. Despite heavy rains, voter turnout was high.

"The people spoke and I will obey them," said Gov. Pedro Rossello, who spearheaded the statehood campaign, in acknowledging defeat in a speech to thousands of supporters.

With all 1,784 pre-cincts reporting, commonwealth received 823,258, or 48.4 percent of the vote; statehood 785,859, or 46.2 percent; independence 75,253, or 4.4 percent.

Supporters of statehood said it would bring billions of dollars in federal aid and played to Puerto Ricans' fears by saying their US citizenship might be lost if they stayed a commonwealth.

But commonwealth supporters contended that the island's culture and language might be lost in statehood and noted that becoming a state would mean Puerto Ricans would have to pay federal taxes.

—*Associated Press*

解答 ☞ p.265

1. Puerto Rico recently voted to
   (A) become the 51st American state.
   (B) become part of a full union with the US.
   (C) remain a US commonwealth.
   (D) enter into a joint government with the US.

2. The results of the ballot showed that
   (A) people in Puerto Rico didn't want to join America.
   (B) people in Puerto Rico did want to join America.
   (C) people agreed with Gov. Pedro Rossello.
   (D) people weren't interested in voting because of heavy rains.

3. Supporters of the statehood campaign believed that
   (A) people would have to pay federal taxes.
   (B) Puerto Rican culture would be lost.
   (C) they would receive billions of dollars in federal aid.
   (D) Puerto Ricans would pay less taxes.

4. Commonwealth supporters contended that
   (A) the island's culture and language would become stronger.
   (B) the island's culture and language might be lost.
   (C) lose their US citizenship.
   (D) crime would increase if they joined the US.

波多黎各人拒絕獨立

波多黎各聖胡安電——波多黎各公民投票揭曉，贊成維持美屬現狀者擊敗主張成爲美國第五十一州者，駁斥了這項本世紀最強的併入美國活動。

昨天的投票顯示，民族尊嚴與經濟因素是選民主要的考量。而且，這是波多黎各二十六年來首次對政治前途舉行公民投票。儘管當天大雨滂沱，投票率仍然很高。

主張成爲美國一州的波多黎各總督羅塞洛，在對幾千位支持者的演說中，承認失敗。他表示：「人民已經決定，我就會遵守。」

在一千七百八十四個選區中，贊成維持美屬現狀者有八十二萬三千二百五十八人，占所有選票的百分之四十八點四；贊成併入美國的有七十八萬五千八百五十九人，占百分之四十六點二；贊成獨立的有七萬五千二百五十三人，占百分之四點四。

主張立州者表示，正式成爲美國一州可以帶來數十億美元的聯邦援助，又針對波人擔心之事指出，若仍維持美屬現狀，可能就會喪失美國公民的身份。

但主張維持現狀者堅決主張，一旦波多黎各成爲美國的一州，本土文化及語言將會喪失，且波境人民將須付聯邦稅。〔美聯社〕

** campaign〔kæm'pen〕*n.* 活動
　commonwealth〔'kɑmən,wɛlθ〕*n.* 共和政體　　***hinge on*** 依～而定
　ethnic〔'ɛθnɪk〕*adj.* 民族的　　ballot〔'bælət〕*n.* 投票
　turnout〔'tɚn,aʊt〕*n.* 出席人數　　spearhead〔'spɪr,hɛd〕*v.* 帶頭
　statehood〔'stethʊd〕*n.* 州的地位
　acknowledge〔ək'nɑlɪdʒ〕*v.* 承認　　precinct〔'prisɪŋkt〕*n.* 地區
　federal〔'fɛdərəl〕*adj.* 美國聯邦政府的
　citizenship〔'sɪtəzn̩,ʃɪp〕*n.* 公民的身份
　contend〔kən'tɛnd〕*v.* 堅決主張

Hijack　　　　　　　　　　　　*Friday Oct. 28*

Public fears impact of hijacks: poll

A majority of people in Taiwan believe the recent hijackings of mainland planes to Taiwan will have an adverse impact on the country's social stability, according to a poll released by an evening newspaper yesterday.

Taipei officials blame the high number of hijackings on poor airport security in the mainland. Beijing points the finger at Taiwan, saying the penalties it imposes on hijackers are too light.

Justice Minister Ma Ying-jeou refuted Beijing's remark that Taiwan imposed light penalties on hijackers, saying that Japan once repatriated a hijacker back to the mainland, who then received a sentence of only eight years in jail.

Meanwhile, an unnamed high-ranking government official told a newspaper yesterday that the reason for such frequent hijackings was because the mainland media only reported Taiwan not repatriating hijackers, without saying that all hijackers were convicted here.

Beijing had blockaded news on Taiwan's sentencing of hijackers because it did not recognize Taiwan as an political entity exercising independent jurisdiction, the official said.

解答☞p.265

1. A majority of people in Taiwan believe hijackings of mainland planes will
   - (A) have a positive effect on the country's social stability.
   - (B) not cause any changes in Taiwan.
   - (C) have a negative effect on Taiwan.
   - (D) be solved by Beijing.

2. Taipei officials blame the hijackings on
   - (A) the high cost of airline tickets.
   - (B) poor security at mainland airports.
   - (C) Japan repatriating a hijacker.
   - (D) the light penalties hijackers receive.

FOCUS

●航空相關字彙
control tower 塔台
runway〔ˈrʌn‚we〕 n. 跑道
emergency landing 緊急降落
cockpit〔ˈkɑk‚pɪt〕 n.;flight deck 駕駛艙
flight data recorder 飛行紀錄儀(黑盒子)

民調顯示：民眾擔憂刼機帶來的衝擊

根據一家晚報昨日公佈的民意調查顯示，多數的台灣人民認為，最近多起刼持大陸飛機來台的事件，會對台灣社會穩定，造成不良的影響。

台北官員將頻繁的刼機事件，歸咎於大陸機場安全檢查的疏失。但北京卻將箭頭指向台灣，認為對刼機犯的懲罰太輕。

對於北京指控台灣對刼機犯懲罰太輕的說法，法務部長馬英九加以反駁，他指出，日本曾遣返一名刼機犯回大陸，結果該名刼機犯只被判了八年的有期徒刑。

同時，一位不願透露姓名的政府高階官員，昨日向一家報紙表示，刼機事件如此頻繁的原因，是大陸媒體只報導台灣不遣返刼機犯，卻沒有報導刼機犯都已被定罪。

這名官員還說，北京方面封鎖消息，是因為中共不承認台灣為具有獨立司法審判權的政治實體。

** impact〔ˈɪmpækt〕*n.* 影響　　hijack〔ˈhaɪˌdʒæk〕*v.* 刼機
poll〔pol〕*n.* 民意調查　　adverse〔ˈædvɝs〕*adj.* 不利的
stability〔stəˈbɪlətɪ〕*n.* 穩定　　***blame ~ on*** … 將～歸咎於…
penalty〔ˈpɛnḷtɪ〕*n.* 懲罰　　impose〔ɪmˈpoz〕*v.* 加（懲罰）於
repatriate〔riˈpetrɪˌet〕*v.* 遣返
media〔ˈmidɪə〕*n.* 媒體　　convict〔kənˈvɪkt〕*v.* 定罪
blockade〔blɑˈked〕*v.* 封鎖　　entity〔ˈɛntətɪ〕*n.* 實體
jurisdiction〔ˌdʒʊrɪsˈdɪkʃən〕*n.* 司法權

英文報紙必備政治用語

◇ diplomat〔'dɪplə,mæt〕*n*. 外交官

◇ ambassador〔æm'bæsədə〕*n*. 大使

◇ foreign affairs 外交事務　diplomatic relations 外交關係

◇ substantial relationship 實質外交

◇ pragmatic diplomacy 務實外交

◇ flexible diplomacy 彈性外交　gunboat diplomacy 武力外交

◇ people's diplomacy 國民外交

◇ most-favored treatment 最惠待遇

◇ franchise〔'fræntʃaɪz〕*n*. 特權

◇ communique〔kə,mjunə'ke〕*n*. 公報

◇ declaration〔,dɛklə'reʃən〕*n*. 宣言

◇ ultimatum〔,ʌltə'metəm〕*n*. 最後通牒

◇ concession〔kən'sɛʃən〕*n*. 讓步

◇ cession〔'sɛʃən〕*n*. （領土的）割讓

◇ trusteeship〔trʌs'tiʃɪp〕*n*. （聯合國的）託管；託管區域

◇ disarmament〔dɪs'ɑrməmənt〕*n*. 裁軍

◇ border dispute 邊界糾紛　bilateral talks 雙邊會談

◇ demilitarization zone 非軍事區

◇ clash〔klæʃ〕*n*. ; conflict〔'kɑnflɪkt〕*n*. 衝突

◇ peacful coexistence 和平共存

◇ truce〔trus〕*n*. 停火（協定）

◇ armed peace 武裝和平　　peace talk 和談

◇ negotiation〔nɪ,goʃɪ'eʃən〕n.；good offices 斡旋

◇ compromise〔'kɑmprə,maɪz〕n. 妥協

◇ arbitration〔,ɑrbə'treʃən〕n. 仲裁

◇ mediation〔,midɪ'eʃn〕n. 調停

◇ conciliation〔kən,sɪlɪ'eʃən〕n. 調解

◇ radical〔'rædɪkl̩〕adj. 急進的　　draft resolution 決議案

◇ summit meeting（talks）高峯會議

◇ draft amendment 修正案　　pullout〔'pʊl,aʊt〕n. 撤退

◇ bill〔bɪl〕n. 議案；法案　　budget〔'bʌdʒɪt〕n. 預算

◇ conservatism〔kən's3vətɪzəm〕n. 保守主義

◇ liberalism〔'lɪbərəl,ɪzəm〕n. 自由主義

◇ nix〔nɪks〕n. 否定　　majority〔mə'dʒɔrətɪ〕n. 多數

◇ intervention〔,ɪntə'vɛnʃən〕n. 干涉；介入

◇ strategy〔'strætədʒɪ〕n. 戰略；對策

◇ minority〔mə'nɔrətɪ,maɪ-〕n. 少數

◇ alliance〔ə'laɪəns〕n. 同盟　　regime〔rɪ'ʒim〕n. 政體

◇ rebellion〔rɪ'bɛljən〕n. 反叛；暴動

◇ candidate〔'kændə,det〕n. 候選人

◇ ballot〔'bælət〕n. 投票

◇ petition〔pə'tɪʃən〕n. 請願；陳情

◇ document〔'dɑkjəmənt〕n. 公文；文件

◇ ratification〔,rætəfə'keʃən〕n. 批准

NAFTA

Wednesday Nov. 19

NAFTA passes easily

Reuter

Washington, Nov. 18 — The U.S. House of Representatives easily passed the key North American Free Trade Agreement (NAFTA) in what President Clinton said was a "defining moment" that would help America shape the 21st century.

The 234-200 vote late on Wednesday means the United States can forge a common market with Mexico and Canada next year and boosts the chances for a world trade treaty by mid-December under the General Agreement on Tariffs and Trade (GATT).

There were celebrations and sighs of relief in Mexico and Canada at the win which will phase out tariffs over 15 years — Mexico has the highest — to allow goods to flow freely.

Canada, where a new Liberal government has threatened to renegotiate NAFTA, was confident it would be able to obtain improvements in the pact to allow it to approve it as well.

European stock markets generally welcomed the news with the NAFTA vote cited by traders as one of a variety of factors pushing up prices.

解答☞ p. 265

1. NAFTA will allow the U.S. to
   (A) bypass Canada and Mexico as trading partners.
   (B) hurt business people in the U.S.
   (C) develop a common market with Mexico and Canada.
   (D) cut back its involvement in world trade.

2. NAFTA was greeted with relief by Mexico and Canada because
   (A) tariffs will be phased out over 15 years.
   (B) they will be able to charge higher prices for goods.
   (C) they can trade with each other and ignore America.
   (D) tariffs will be increased over 15 years.

3. The Canadian government has said that it will
   (A) reject NAFTA.
   (B) try and obtain improvements in the pact so it can approve it.
   (C) approve NAFTA immediately.
   (D) need to discuss the deal with Mexico.

4. European stock markets reacted to the NAFTA vote by
   (A) welcoming it.
   (B) fearing it will cause problems in Japan.
   (C) closing the stock exchanges for one day.
   (D) letting a fall in prices occur.

北美自由貿易協定輕易過關

〔路透社〕華盛頓十一月十八日電——關鍵性的北美自由貿易協定在美國眾議院輕易過關，柯林頓總統指其為「決定的一刻」，將有助於美國建構廿一世紀的藍圖。

此協定於週三稍晚以二百卅四票對二百票通過，這表示美國將於明年和墨西哥、及加拿大組成一共同市場，而且關貿總協之下的新世界貿易協定，於十二月中旬前通過的機會，也將增加。

墨西哥和加拿大為投票獲勝而慶祝，並鬆了一口氣，尤其是關稅最高的墨西哥。在未來十五年，三國間將逐步取消關稅，使貨物能自由流通。

在加拿大，新成立的自由政府曾強硬要求重新商議協定內容，但加國確信協定將獲得改善，並贊同協定的通過。

大致而言，這項消息受到歐洲股市的歡迎。交易商將北美貿協的通過，視為提昇股市價格的多項因素之一。

** Representative 〔ˌrɛprɪˈzɛntətɪv〕 *n.* 〔美〕眾議員
North American Free Trade Agreement 北美自由貿易協定
　　（簡稱 ***NAFTA***）
forge 〔fɔrdʒ, fordʒ〕 *v.* 籌劃；策略
boost 〔bust〕 *v.* 增加；提高　　　treaty 〔ˈtritɪ〕 *n.* 協商；協定
General Agreement on Tariffs and Trade 關稅貿易總協
　　（簡稱 ***GATT***）
phase out 逐步廢止　　　tariff 〔ˈtærɪf〕 *n.* 關稅
renegotiate 〔ˌrinɪˈgoʃɪˌet〕 *v.* 再協商

Monday Jan. 10

Peace deal to be signed 'soon'

Switzerland — Israeli Foreign Minister Shimon Peres and PLO leader Yasser Arafat were reported close to agreement yesterday on final terms for an Israeli withdrawal from the Gaza Strip and Jericho.

Optimism about a breakthrough grew as evening talks at a luxury hotel in this Alpine resort progressed.

The two sides reportedly presented new maps and proposals to tackle contentious issues, including how much area around the West Bank town of Jericho will be ceded to the Palestinians.

Israel demands it maintain security on the borders, but the PLO says the presence of Israeli soldiers would violate the guarantees of autonomy.

Arafat and Peres are due to join a debate on Middle East peace yesterday with Egypt's foreign minister and Jordan's crown prince at the privately organized World Economic Forum. The aim apparently seems to be to announce the deal at that afternoon session.

Associated Press

解答 ☞ p.265

1. Israeli Foreign Minister Shimon Peres and PLO leader Yasser Arafat were reported to be
   (A) on close terms and planning a holiday in Jericho.
   (B) disagreeing over the terms of Israeli withdrawal.
   (C) on bad terms over the Israeli withdrawal from the Gaza Strip.
   (D) close to agreement on the terms for Israel's withdrawal.

2. In the talks, Israel demanded that it should be able to
   (A) retain its troops and security on the borders.
   (B) install security alarm systems on its borders.
   (C) have all border soldiers returned to Israel.
   (D) ignore all PLO requests.

3. Arafat and Peres were scheduled to debate
   (A) tourism in the Middle East.
   (B) Middle East peace.
   (C) the advantages of the World Economic Forum.
   (D) the role of royalty in Egypt and Jordan.

FOCUS

以色列與巴勒斯坦解放組織經過漫長艱苦的談判
後，已簽署了歷史性的巴人局部自治協定，正式
賦予在加薩走廊與耶律戈境內巴勒斯坦人自治的
權力。使他們重獲一九六七年中東戰後失去的自
由，並向巴勒斯坦獨立建國邁進一大步。

和平協議卽將簽署

　　瑞士電——據報導，以色列外長培瑞斯和巴解領導人阿拉法特，昨針對以色列自加薩走廊及耶律戈撤退的最後條件，幾近達成協議。

　　會議昨晚在阿爾卑斯山渡假勝地的一間豪華旅館進行，整個會議對於突破難關顯現出樂觀的氣氛。

　　爲解決引起爭論的問題，據報導雙方皆提出了新地圖及提議。包括約旦河西岸的耶律戈周圍，該割讓多少土地給巴勒斯坦人。

　　以色列要求維持邊境的安全部隊，但巴解組織表示，以軍的出現會違反自治的保證。

　　阿拉法特和培瑞斯昨日預定要參加私下組成的世界經濟討論會，和埃及外長及約旦王子討論中東和平問題，其目的顯然是要宣布當日下午會中達成的協議。〔美聯社〕

** Switzerland〔'swɪtsələnd〕*n.* 瑞士
　　Israeli〔ɪz'relɪ〕*adj.* 以色列的
　　PLO 巴勒斯坦解放組織（*the Palestine Liberation Organization*）
　　withdraw〔wɪθ'drɔ〕*v.* 撤退　　Gaza Strip 加薩走廊
　　Jericho〔'dʒɛrə,ko〕*n.* 耶律戈（巴勒斯坦之古城）
　　optimism〔'ɑptə,mɪzəm〕*n.* 樂觀主義
　　breakthrough〔'brek,θru〕*n.* 突破（難關）
　　luxury〔'lʌkʃərɪ〕*adj.* 豪華的
　　Alpine〔'ælpaɪn〕*adj.* 阿爾卑斯山的
　　resort〔rɪ'zɔrt〕*n.* 旅遊勝地　　proposal〔prə'pozḷ〕*n.* 提議
　　tackle〔'tækḷ〕*v.* 解決

What is Kurdistan?

何謂「庫德斯坦」?

Kurdistan, a region rich in oil and water and strategically important to Turks, Arabs and Persians, is the homeland of most of the world's 25 million Kurds. Globally the Kurdish people are one of the largest ethnic groups without a country of its own.

庫德斯坦是一個盛產石油、水源充沛的地區，而且是土耳其人、阿拉伯人和波斯人的戰略要地。它是全世界二十五萬庫德族人的家園。庫德人是全世界沒有國家的最大一族。

Daily patrols by military planes from the United States, Great Britain, France and Turkey have protected the Kurds from Iraqi attacks.

每天都有來自美國、英國、法國和土耳其的軍機在上空巡邏，保護庫德族免於伊拉克人的攻擊。

The flights cover the security zone established in Iraq north of the 36 th parallel after the Persian Gulf War.

這些軍機飛行的區域，是波斯灣戰爭後，設於伊拉克境內北緯三十六度以北的安全區。

＊＊ Kurdistan〔͵kɝdɪˈstæn〕 *n.* 庫德斯坦
　　strategically〔strəˈtidʒɪkəlɪ〕 *adv.* 戰略上
　　Kurd〔kɝd〕 *n.* 庫德人　　ethnic〔ˈɛθnɪk〕 *adj.* 種族的
　　patrol〔pəˈtrol〕 *n.* 巡邏

ROC plan for F-16s broadened

*The China Post
and Reuter*

Taiwan will offer to repair F-16 jet fighters for its Asian neighbors after the island builds a center to maintain the 150 F-16s it is buying, a senior aerospace official said yesterday.

"In the long term we will seek such business, though it will depend on whether it is economically efficient and whether our technical standard is high enough," said deputy director of the ministerial Committee for Aviation and Space Industry Development.

He declined to name specific customers for the center, but the local Central News Agency said Taiwan would ask South Korea, Malaysia, Singapore and Saudi Arabia to send its F-16s to the facility for repairs.

Under a pact signed last July, the plane's maker, Lockheed Corp., agreed to help Taiwan establish a facility to maintain the 150 F-16 jet fighters that Taipei last year agreed to buy for about US $6 billion. Delivery is expected to begin around 1996.

解答 ☞ p. 265

1. It has been reported that Taiwan will offer to
   (A) repatriate hijackers in F-16 jets.
   (B) research F-16 jet fighter designs for its Asian neighbors.
   (C) fix F-16 jet fighters for Asian neighbors.
   (D) reject F-16 jet fighters that are unsuitable for Asian neighbors.

2. The Taiwan facility would
   (A) teach students how to be pilots.
   (B) maintain and repair F-16 jet fighters.
   (C) be unable to repair an entire F-16.
   (D) not help repair F-16s for South Korea, Malaysia, Singapore and Saudi Arabia.

3. Lockheed Corp has agreed to help Taiwan
   (A) build a US $ 6 billion facility.
   (B) set up a facility to maintain F-16 jet fighters.
   (C) build F-16 jet fighters from scratch.
   (D) look for business deals in South Korea, Malaysia, Singapore, and Saudi Arabia.

 *FOCUS*

中華民國建立F-16 戰機維修中心後，如果能提高私人投資，再加上政府積極參與，該中心將成爲除美國外，第一所能修理整架F-16 的修護地。

中華民國將擴大F-16計劃

〔中國郵報；路透社〕一位航太高級官員昨天表示，在替所購買的一百五十架F-16戰鬥機建立維修中心之後，台灣將提供亞洲鄰近國家修理F-16戰鬥機的服務。

航太工業發展委員會副會長表示，儘管必須考慮經濟效益以及本身科技水準是否夠高等問題，長遠看來，我們仍會做這樣的生意。

他拒絕透露該中心的客戶名單。但據本地的中央新聞社指出，台灣會要求南韓、馬來西亞、新加坡，以及沙烏地阿拉伯將F-16戰鬥機送來維修。

根據去年七月所簽訂的合約，F-16的製造商—洛克希德公司同意幫台灣建立維修設施，以修護去年花費六十億美元購買的一百五十架F-16戰鬥機。預計大約1966年會開始將設備運送來台。

** maintain〔men′ten〕v. 維修
aerospace〔′ɛrə,spes〕adj. 航空與太空的
in the long term 就長期而言　　deputy〔′dɛpjətɪ〕adj. 副…
aviation〔,evɪ′eʃən〕n. 飛行
complement〔′kɑmpləmənt〕v. 補充
decline〔dɪ′klaɪn〕v. 拒絕　　facility〔fə′sɪlətɪ〕n. 設備
pact〔pækt〕n. 契約；協定

英文報紙必備軍事用語

◇ commission 〔kə'mıʃən〕 *n*. 軍官的任命；軍官的地位

◇ army 〔'ɑrmɪ〕 *n*. 陸軍　　navy 〔'nevɪ〕 *n*. 海軍

◇ air force　空軍　　chief of the general staff　參謀總長

◇ top brass　高級軍官 (俗稱)

◇ military spokesman　軍事發言人

◇ cock off　走火　　parade 〔pə'red〕 *n*. 閱兵

◇ volunteer 〔,vɑlən'tır〕 *n*. 志願兵

◇ draft 〔dræft〕; conscription 〔kən'skrıpʃən〕 *n*. 徵兵

◇ compulsory military service　義務服役

◇ balance of power　均勢 (軍力平衡)

◇ maneuver 〔mə'nuvə〕 *n*. 策略　　*v*. 演習

◇ pillow fight　作戰演習　　military installations　軍事設施

◇ clash 〔klæʃ〕 *n*. 衝突　　area at issue　紛爭地區

◇ armed intervention　武力干涉

◇ invasion 〔ın've3ən〕 *n*. 侵略

◇ civil war　內戰　　fuse 〔fjuz〕 *n*. 導火線

◇ declaration of war　宣戰

◇ military target　軍事目標

◇ front line　前線　　line of battle　戰線

◇ base 〔bes〕 *n*. 基地

◇ strategy 〔'strætəd3ı〕 *n*. (全盤性的) 戰略

◇ tactics〔'tæktɪks〕*n.*（個別戰鬥上的）戰術

◇ nuclear test　核子試爆

◇ reconnaissance〔rɪ'kɑnəsəns〕*n.* 偵察

◇ fire power　火力　　truce〔trus〕*n.* 停火；休戰

◇ captive〔'kæptɪv〕*n.* 戰俘

◇ POW（prisoner of war）戰犯

◇ ammunition〔,æmjə'nɪʃən〕*n.* 軍火

◇ weapon〔'wɛpən〕*n.* 武器　　nuclear weapons　核子武器

- -

◇ missile〔'mɪsḷ〕*n.* 飛彈

◇ war head　彈頭　　guided missile　導向飛彈

◇ atomic bomb　原子彈　　nuclear bomb　核子彈

◇ tank〔tæŋk〕*n.* 坦克車　　armored vehicle　裝甲車

◇ machine gun　機關槍　　hand grenade　手榴彈

◇ arms depot　軍火庫

◇ fighter〔'faɪtɚ〕*n.* 戰鬥機

◇ bomber〔'bɑmɚ〕*n.* 轟炸機

- -

◇ MIG（27、29、31…）米格機（蘇）

◇ reconnaissance plane；U 2（TR-1）偵察機

◇ helicopter〔'hɛlɪ,kɑptɚ, 'hi-〕*n.* 直升機

◇ aircraft carrier　航空母艦（簡稱為 carrier）

◇ cruiser〔'kruzɚ〕*n.* 巡洋艦

◇ submarine〔'sʌbmə,rin, ,sʌbmə'rin〕*n.* 潛水艇（簡稱為 sub）

Legislation

Friday Jan. 7

New law enacted to back shoppers

By Alice Hung
The China Post

The Legislature yesterday completed final approval of Taiwan's first Consumer Protection Law, providing unprecedented legal protection to local consumers ranging from home-buying to water bills.

President Lee Tung-hui promulgated the law last night, putting it into effect.

The law applies to all consumers, ROC citizens and alien residents alike. It allows consumers for the first time to seek compensation for defective goods and services even if there is no evidence of negligence or intent to harm on the part of the designers, manufacturers or providers.

Under the newly enacted law, designers, manufacturers and providers of services are liable to consumers for the safety and quality of their products and services.

Violators of the law now face fines of up to NT$1.5 million as well as jail sentences under criminal statutes.

解答 ☞ p. 265

1. Taiwan's first Consumer Protection Law provides
   (A) for shopkeepers to legally overcharge customers.
   (B) no legal protection for consumers.
   (C) home owners with services at lower prices.
   (D) unprecedented legal protection for local consumers.

2. The Consumer Protection Law allows consumers
   (A) to harm the designers of defective products.
   (B) to pay less for consumer items.
   (C) to seek compensation for defective goods and services.
   (D) no compensation for defective goods and services.

3. Under the new law, manufacturers are liable to
   (A) consumers for the safety and quality of their products.
   (B) manufacture shoddy goods.
   (C) provide minimal service.
   (D) increase prices for services.

4. Violators of the law will face
   (A) no criminal charges.
   (B) fines of up to $1.5 million and jail.
   (C) being paid $1.5 billion.
   (D) being turned into statues.

新法頒佈——購物者有保障

〔中國郵報〕立法院昨天三讀通過國內第一條消費者保護法，提供本地消費者法律上之保障，其範圍包括家庭用品之購買，乃至於水費等等。

李總統登輝先生昨天晚上頒佈了這項法令，並且立即實施。

這項法律適用於所有的消費者，包括中華民國國民與外籍居民。使得消費者第一次有機會申訴。即使沒有證據證明商品設計者、製造者、或提供服務者是有意或無意造成傷害，消費者都有機會為有瑕疵的商品與不良的服務索賠。

這項新法頒佈之後，無論是商品設計者、製造業者，或是提供服務者都必須在商品或服務安全與品質方面，對消費者負責任。

現在，違反這項新法的人最高將被處以新台幣一百五十萬元之罰鍰，而且也會被判刑。

** enact〔ɪnˈækt〕v. 制定；頒佈　　back〔bæk〕v. 支持；擁護
legislature〔ˈlɛdʒɪsˌletʃə〕n. 立法機關
unprecedented〔ʌnˈprɛsəˌdɛntɪd〕adj. 無先例的
promulgate〔prəˈmʌlget〕v. 公佈
put sth. into effect 實施~　　***apply to*** 適用於
alien〔ˈelɪən, -ljən〕adj. 外國的　　resident〔ˈrɛzədənt〕n. 居民
compensation〔ˌkɑmpənˈseʃən〕n. 賠償
defective〔dɪˈfɛktɪv〕adj. 有缺點的
negligence〔ˈnɛglədʒəns〕n. 疏忽
manufacturer〔ˌmænjəˈfæktʃərə〕n. 製造業者
be liable to~　對~有責任　　violator〔ˈvaɪəˌletə〕n. 違反者
fine〔faɪn〕n. 罰金　　sentence〔ˈsɛntəns〕n. 判決
statute〔ˈstætʃʊt〕n. 成文法；法規

Official policy

ROC says one China still policy

By Christopher Bodeen
Special to The China Post

The Ministry of Foreign Affairs yesterday reacted to comments by Economics Minister P.K. Chiang on Sunday that Taiwan and mainland China are for the time being two separate sovereign states — the first diversion from the official one China policy by a ranking government offical.

"Before the conditions for reunification are ripe, the government will be pragmatic and adopt a so-called two Chinas policy at this stage with one China as its ultimate goal," Chiang said in a prepared statement before a press conference in Seattle where he represented the ROC in trade talks at the Asia Pacific Economic Cooperation forum.

Chiang continued that the ROC is a sovereign nation, not a province of the People's Republic of China.

But Foreign Minister Fredrick Chien yesterday said Chiang's comments do not represent a change in official policy. He said they were merely a reaction to increasing hostility from Beijing, including moves by the mainland to block the ROC's application to rejoin the United Nations.

解答☞ p. 265

1. Economics Minister P.K. Chiang commented that
   (A) China and Taiwan are one nation.
   (B) ROC is a province of the People's Republic of China.
   (C) Taiwan and mainland China are separate sovereign states.
   (D) the goal of one China has been achieved.

2. Chiang believes that before conditions are ripe for reunification, the government will
   (A) adopt a two Chinas policy.
   (B) launch a campaign of resistance to China.
   (C) make no attempt to achieve the goal of one China.
   (D) attempt to achieve the ultimate goal of two Chinas.

3. Foreign Minister Frederick Chien said Chiang's comments
   (A) represent a change in official policy.
   (B) show that he supports mainland policy.
   (C) don't represent a change in official policy.
   (D) were made because he was hostile towards the United Nations.

中華民國表示一個中國的政策不變

〔中國郵報〕經濟部長江丙坤於週日評論指出，台灣與中國大陸爲階段性的兩個主權國家，這是第一次由政府高階官員所發表，有異於官方一個中國政策的說法。昨日外交部做出回應。

此次江丙坤代表中華民國參加亞太經合會貿易談判，他在西雅圖的記者會上表示：「在統一的條件成熟之前，政府會以務實的態度，在此一階段採取兩個中國政策，以達到一個中國的終極目標。」

江丙坤並指出，中華民國是一主權國家，絕非中華人民共和國的一個省分。

但是，外交部長錢復昨日表示，江丙坤的說法並不表示官方政策有所改變。並說這只是爲了反駁北京方面愈來愈多的敵意，其中包括了中共企圖阻止我國申請重返聯合國的行動。

** The Ministry of Foreign Affairs 外交部
Economics Minister 經濟部長
sovereign〔'savrɪn〕*adj.* 有主權的　　diversion〔daɪ'vɜʒən〕*n.* 轉變
reunification〔,rijunəfə'keʃən〕*n.* 再統一
ripe〔raɪp〕*adj.* 成熟的　　pragmatic〔præg'mætɪk〕*adj.* 務實的
ultimate〔'ʌltəmɪt〕*adj.* 最後的
Asia Pacific Economic Cooperation 亞太經濟合作（簡稱 *APEC*）
forum〔'fɔrəm〕*n.* 討論會　　Foreign Minister 外交部長
hostility〔has'tɪlətɪ〕*n.* 敵意　　block〔blak〕*v.* 阻止
application〔,æplə'keʃən〕*n.* 申請
rejoin〔rɪ'dʒɔɪn〕*v.* 再加入

NATO

Wednesday Jan. 12

NATO reaches out to East

Reuter

Brussels, Jan. 11 —NATO leaders ended a summit on Tuesday, hailing a new era for their 45-year-old alliance and offering a new partnership to former Warsaw Pact foes, but only papering over differences on the war in Bosnia.

The final declaration affirmed the North Atlantic Treaty Organization's readiness to admit new members from Eastern Europe, although it set no date.

"We expect and would welcome NATO expansion that would reach out to democratic states in our East, as part of an evolutionary process, taking into account political and security developments in the whole of Europe," the declaration said.

解答☞ p. 265

1. The NATO summit resulted in

(A) the end of a 45-year-old alliance.

(B) arguments with former Warsaw Pact foes.

(C) papers on Bosnia's future being signed.

(D) a new era for the 45-year-old alliance.

2. The NATO declaration stated that

(A) it was ready to admit new members from Eastern Europe.

(B) it had set the date to admit Eastern European members.

(C) it was not interested in expansion into the democratic states in the East.

(D) it would never admit members from Eastern Europe.

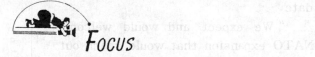

FOCUS

● 世界組織

WTO (World Trade Organization)
世界貿易組織

APEC (Asian Pacific Economic Cooperation) 亞太經合會

EC (European Community)
歐洲共同體

ASEAN (Association of Southeast Asian Nations) 東南亞國協

北約觸及東歐

〔路透社〕布魯塞爾，一月十一日電——北大西洋公約組織各國領袖的高峯會議於週四結束，此次會議爲他們四十五年來陳舊的同盟關係開創了一個新局面，也讓前華沙公約中的敵國能夠加入，但卻隱瞞了對波士尼亞內戰的不同觀點。

最後的宣言雖沒有訂定日期，但可以肯定的是，北大西洋公約組織已準備好吸收東歐新進的會員。

宣言聲明，「我們盼望也歡迎北約組織的擴展能成爲進步過程的一部分，使其能觸及東歐的民主國家，以對我們整個歐洲政治及安全的發展加以注意。」

** *NATO* 北大西洋公約組織
    (*North Atlantic Treaty Organization*)
    summit〔'sʌmit〕*n.* 高峯會議
    alliance〔ə'laɪəns〕*n.* 同盟
    partnership〔'partnɚ,ʃɪp〕*n.* 合夥關係
    Warsaw Pact 華沙公約　　***paper over*** 掩飾；隱瞞
    Bosnia〔'bɑznɪə〕*n.* 波士尼亞
    declaration〔,dɛklə'reʃən〕*n.* 宣言
    evolutionary〔,ɛvə'luʃən,ɛrɪ〕*adj.* 發展的
    take sth. into account 對某事物加以注意考慮

Cross-strait ties

Koo says Beijing trip OK

*By **Alice Hung** The China Post and agencies*

Koo Chen-fu, chairman of the Straits Exchange Foundation (SEF), said he would accept an invitation to Beijing, but the supervisory Mainland Affairs Council does not think so.

Wang Daohan asked Koo to come to Beijing between Spring and Summer.

Three rounds of functional talks at the deputy secretary-general level ended futile last year. Chiao expressed earlier that he hopes the Chiao-Tang talks will facilitate a fourth round of functional talks.

During the ongoing Chiao-Tang talks in Beijing, SEF and ARATS yesterday agreed in principle to set up mediation centers on both sides to settle cross-strait fishing disputes.

But disagreements on the repatriation of hijackers and illegal immigrants persisted, as neither side was willing to give ground on politically sensitive issues involving legal jurisdiction.

解答 ☞ p.265

1. What does Koo Chen-fu think about the possibility of exchange visits?

   (A) They should depend on the results of ongoing negotiations.

   (B) They should depend on the good will of Beijing.

   (C) He sees no obstacles to visits by either side.

   (D) He thinks the Mainland Affairs Council should decide.

2. What happened at the previous rounds of deputy secretary-general level functional talks?

   (A) They led to the possibility of exchange visits.

   (B) They were unable to achieve anything.

   (C) They led Koo Chen-fu to feel optimistic about future talks.

   (D) They mediated fishing disputes.

3. What did the two sides fail to agree on at the ongoing talks?

   (A) The need for exchange visits.

   (B) The solution to cross-straight fishing disputes.

   (C) The way to set up mediation centers for hijackers.

   (D) How to send back hijackers and illegal immigrants.

4. Why did the talks fail on certain issues?

   (A) They were too sensitive to discuss.

   (B) They involved questions of legal authority.

   (C) The problems only happened to Taiwan.

   (D) Neither side acknowledged the problems.

辜振甫同意赴北京訪問

〔中國郵報〕海基會董事長辜振甫表示將接受訪問北京之邀請，但負責監督的陸委會並不這麼認為。

汪道涵邀請辜振甫於春夏之交赴北京訪問。

去年兩會所舉行的三回合副秘書長級的事務性談判，並無任何重大突破。焦仁和稍早表示，他希望焦唐會談能促使第四回合事務性會談的召開。

正在北京進行的焦唐會談中，海基會和海協會昨同意雙方設定調處中心的原則，以解決漁事糾紛。

但當談到有關司法審判權的敏感性政治問題時，雙方都不願意讓步，所以，遣返劫機犯及偷渡客的問題，雙方仍然僵持不下。

** the Straits Exchange Foundation (*SEF*) 海峽兩岸交流基金會
    （簡稱海基會）
supervisory 〔,supə'vaɪzərɪ 〕*adj.* 監督的
the Mainland Affairs Council 大陸事務委員會（簡稱陸委會）
deputy 〔'dɛpjətɪ 〕*adj.* 副⋯
futile 〔'fjutl 〕*adj.* 徒勞的
facilitate 〔fə'sɪlə,tet 〕*v.* 幫助；使容易
mediation 〔,midɪ'eʃən 〕*n.* 仲裁；調停
dispute 〔dɪ'spjut 〕*v.* 爭論
repatriation 〔ri'petrɪ,eʃən 〕*n.* 遣返
hijacker 〔'haɪdʒækə(r) 〕*n.* 劫機犯
immigrant 〔'ɪməgrənt 〕*n.* 移民（自外國移入）
give ground 讓步
jurisdiction 〔,dʒʊrɪs'dɪkʃən 〕*n.* 司法權；裁判權

Part 4

Sports & Entertainment 體育娛樂

Saturday Mar. 12

Date downs Martinez

MELBOURNE — Ambidextrous Kimiko Date, urged on by cheering, flag-waving compatriots, delivered a left-right combination yesterday to oust No. 3 seed Conchita Martinez from the quarterfinals of the Australian Open women's singles.

The Japanese fans, many of them with faces painted with the red and white Japanese flag, repeatedly called out to Date to show courage.

Date switched her racket from hand to hand and downed the Spaniard 6-2, 4-6, 6-3 to become only the second Japanese woman to make a singles semifinal at a Grand Slam tournament.

Date, who is naturally left-handed, began playing tennis as a right-hander but hit a handful of shots with her left hand during the match — most of them successful.

Date, the 23-year-old No.10 seed from Tokyo, stretched her winning streak to 10 matches. Earlier this month she won the New South Wales Open in Sydney, moving into the top 10 in the rankings for the first time.

解答 ☞ p.265

1. Date beat Martinez by
   (A) playing as a right-hander.
   (B) delivering a left-right combination.
   (C) playing with her left hand.
   (D) the help of a Spanish player.

2. What is unusual about Date's playing style ?
   (A) She can play with either hand.
   (B) She hits the ball so hard.
   (C) She was able to stretch her winning streak.
   (D) She has a positive attitude about deep groundstrokes.

3. After Date won the New South Wales Open, she
   (A) was able to make a singles semifinal at a Grand Slam tournament.
   (B) became left-handed.
   (C) moved into the top 10 in the rankings.
   (D) was ousted from the quarterfinals of the Australian Open women's singles.

4. What is remarkable about Date's success ?
   (A) She is 23.
   (B) She won the New South Wales Open.
   (C) She is only the second Japanese to reach this stage in a big tournament.
   (D) She had a lot of supporters from Japan.

伊達公子擊敗瑪汀妮茲

墨爾本電——受到熱情的球迷揮舞國旗給予鼓勵，雙手萬能的伊達公子昨天在澳洲公開賽女子單打中，展現了左右開攻的球技，將第三種子球員瑪汀妮茲從複賽中淘汰出局。

許多日本球迷臉上塗著紅白國旗，不斷地叫喊以激勵伊達公子的士氣。

伊達以不斷換手持拍的方式，擊敗了西班牙籍對手，比數為6比2、4比6、及6比3，並成為有始以來第二位打進大滿貫單打準決賽的日本女選手。

伊達本來是左撇子，在開始打網球時卻以右手持拍，但在比賽中又常以左手揮拍得分——大都是成功的攻擊。

年僅二十三歲，來自東京的第十種子伊達，已連勝了十場。早在本月初，她在雪梨贏得了新南威爾斯公開賽女子單打冠軍，使她的世界排名首次進入前十名。

** compatriot 〔kəmˊpetrɪət〕 n. 同胞
combination 〔ˌkɑmbəˊneʃən〕 n. 結合
oust 〔aʊst〕 v. 趕走　　quarterfinal 〔ˌkwɔrtɚˊfaɪnḷ〕 n. 複賽
Australian Open 澳洲公開賽　　single 〔ˊsɪŋgḷ〕 n. 單打
fan 〔fæn〕 n. (電影、運動等的)迷　　switch 〔swɪtʃ〕 v. 變換
racket 〔ˊrækɪt〕 n. (網球、羽毛球等的) 球拍
semifinal 〔ˌseməˊfaɪnḷ〕 n. 準決賽
tournament 〔ˊtʊrnəmənt, ˊtɝ-〕 n. 錦標賽
left-handed 〔ˊlɛftˊhændɪd〕 adj. 左撇子的
handful 〔ˊhænd, fʊl〕 n. 一握　　streak 〔strik〕 n. 一連串
Sydney 〔ˊsɪdnɪ〕 n. 雪梨

Movie

'Mei Chen' wins at San Diego Film Festival

" Mei Chen, " a movie scripted and directed by Liu Chia-chang, took five awards at the First San Diego International Film Festival in San Diego, California. Liu represented the Republic of China.

The film won honors for best feature film, best director, best actress, best music and best theme song.

Of the twelve movies nominated for the top award, " Mei Chen " was an early favorite along with a Russian motion picture titled " Little Angel, Make a Joy " and an Argentine film called " Naked Tango. "

The film festival organizers also announced beforehand that the lifetime achievement award was being given to Mickey Rooney.

解答 ☞ p. 265

1. What does nominate mean ?
   (A) to collect   (B) to consider
   (C) to award   (D) to put forward

2. Where did Mei Chen's principal competition come from?
   (A) Argentina and Russia   (B) San Diego and Tango
   (C) Twelve movies   (D) Mickey Rooney

「梅珍」聖地牙哥影展獲獎

　　由劉家昌自編自導的影片「梅珍」，代表中華民國在加州聖地牙哥國際影展獲得了五大獎項。

　　本片榮獲最佳影片、最佳導演、最佳女主角、最佳音樂以及最佳主題曲。

　　十二部提名角逐首獎的電影中，「梅珍」和蘇聯電影「快樂吧！天使」，以及阿根廷電影「赤裸的探戈」都是原先獲得青睞的作品。

　　影展創辦人亦於會前宣布終生成就獎，由米奇·魯尼獲得。

** festival 〔ˈfɛstəvl〕 *n.* 文化性活動　　script 〔skrɪpt〕 *v.* 寫劇本
　 direct 〔dəˈrɛkt〕 *v.* 導演　　award 〔əˈwɔrd〕 *n.* 獎
　 nominate 〔ˈnɑmə,net〕 *v.* 提名
　 Russian 〔ˈrʌʃən〕 *adj.* 俄國的
　 Argentine 〔ˈɑrdʒən,taɪn〕 *adj.* 阿根廷的
　 organizer 〔ˈɔrgən,aɪzɚ〕 *n.* 創辦者；組織者
　 announce 〔əˈnaʊns〕 *v.* 宣布
　 beforehand 〔bɪˈfor,hænd〕 *adv.* 事前

Super cup

Friday Feb. 25

Cowboys win 2nd straight title

ATLANTA—The Cowboys won their second straight NFL championship and were proclaimed the team of the '90s. The Bills lost in the title game for the fourth straight time, something no team has ever done in any sport.

Dallas found its spark in two unlikely stars, James Washington and Leon Lett.

Washington, a backup safety, had a hand in 17 of Dallas' points as they beat the Bills for the second year in a row, this time 30-13. By becoming four-time losers, the Bills did what no franchise in history has ever done — lose a championship game four straight times.

The most important of those turnovers was the work of Lett, who stripped Thomas of the ball on the third play of the second half with Buffalo holding a 13-6 lead.

Washington, whose interception led to Dallas' first touchdown in last year's 52-17 rout of Buffalo, picked it up and rambled in for the touchdown that tied the game, changed the momentum forever and guaranteed Buffalo its place in NFL history.

Associated Press

解答☞ p. 265

1. Why were Dallas and Buffalo playing for Superbowl history ?

(A) Neither had been in the Superbowl before.

(B) Both had won three times.

(C) The Bills had lost four times in a row, Dallas had won two times.

(D) Both were trying to be the "Team of the 90s."

2. Who gave Dallas its spark ?

(A) Two players not previously considered stars

(B) Two star players

(C) Two stars who had not been likely to play

(D) Two players who scored 17 of Dallas' points

3. Buffalo's defeat was

(A) unprecedented.　　(B) unlikely.

(C) previous.　　(D) innaugural.

FOCUS

● 美式足球相關字彙

gridiron 〔'grɪd,aɪən〕 n. 美式足球球場

goal 〔gol〕 n. 球門　　ten yards line 十碼線

kick off 開球　grounding ball 壓球觸地

direct touch 直接觸地

penalty kick 罰踢

牛仔隊蟬連超級盃冠軍

亞特蘭大電──牛仔隊贏得了連續第二個國家聯盟冠軍，並被喻為「九○年的代表隊伍」。比爾隊則連續第四次在超級盃冠軍賽中失利，是各項運動中史無前例的紀錄。

達拉斯牛仔隊在這次比賽中出現兩匹黑馬──詹姆士‧華盛頓和里恩‧列特。

華盛頓是候補安全衛，他在此次比賽中獨得十七分，最後牛仔隊以30比13連續第二次擊敗比爾隊。水牛城比爾隊則四度輸掉冠軍賽，成為聯盟隊伍中，唯一連續四年打入決賽都吃敗仗的隊伍。

下半場第三節時，比爾隊以13比6領先，但牛仔隊的列特迫使比爾隊的湯馬斯失球，是這場比賽的關鍵。

此時，華盛頓拾起球並獨跑完成達陣，將比數追成13平，情勢因而逆轉，奠定了水牛城比爾隊在國家聯盟歷史中的地位。而去年牛仔隊以52比17擊敗比爾隊的比賽中，華盛頓也是在攔截後完成了第一次達陣。〔美聯社〕

** NFL 國家美式足球聯盟 (*National Football League*)
championship 〔ˈtʃæmpɪənˌʃɪp〕 *n*. 錦標賽
proclaim 〔proˈklem〕 *v*. 宣布　　backup 〔ˈbækˌʌp〕 *adj*. 候補的
safety 〔ˈseftɪ〕 *n*. 安全衛；(美式足球)安全得分
in a row 連續地　　franchise 〔ˈfræntʃaɪz〕 *n*. 加盟權
turnover 〔ˈtɚnˌ ovɚ〕 *n*. 轉機　　Buffalo 〔ˈbʌflˌo〕 *n*. 水牛城
interception 〔ˌɪntɚˈsɛpʃən〕 *n*. 攔截
touchdown 〔ˈtʌtʃˌdaʊn〕 *n*. 達陣；觸地得分
ramble 〔ˈræmblˌ〕 *v*. 漫步
momentum 〔moˈmɛntəm〕 *n*. 情勢
guarantee 〔ˌgærənˈti〕 *v*. 保證

英文報紙必備體育用語

◇ athletics〔æθ'lɛtɪks〕*n*. 體育

◇ coach〔kotʃ〕*n*. 教練　　serve〔sɜv〕*v*. 發球

◇ football〔'fʊt,bɔl〕*n*. 橄欖球；足球

◇ American football 美式足球　　soccer〔'sɑkɚ〕*n*. 足球

◇ basketball〔'bæskɪt,bɔl〕*n*. 籃球

◇ volleyball〔'vɑlɪ,bɔl〕*n*. 排球

◇ baseball〔'bes'bɔl〕*n*. 棒球　　tennis〔'tɛnɪs〕*n*. 網球

◇ handball〔'hænd,bɔl〕*n*. 手球　　polo〔'polo〕*n*. 馬球

◇ badminton〔'bædmɪntən〕*n*. 羽毛球

◇ bowling〔'bolɪŋ〕*n*. 保齡球

◇ golf〔gɑlf,gɔlf〕*n*. 高爾夫球　　boxing〔'bɑksɪŋ〕*n*. 拳擊

◇ billiards〔'bɪljɚdz〕*n*. 撞球

◇ calisthenics〔,kæləs'θɛnɪks〕*n*. 體操

◇ wrestling〔'rɛslɪŋ〕*n*. 摔角；相撲

◇ judo〔'dʒudo〕*n*. 柔道　　sumo〔'sumo〕*n*. 相撲；角力

◇ national gymnastics 國術　　track and field 田徑

◇ cycling〔'saɪklɪŋ〕*n*. 騎自行車

◇ archery〔'ɑrtʃərɪ〕*n*. 箭術

◇ horsemanship〔'hɔrsmən,ʃɪp〕*n*. 馬術

◇ ace〔es〕*n*. （網球賽、排球賽的）發球得分

◇ spectator〔'spɛktetɚ〕*n*. 觀衆

◇ standing〔'stændɪŋ〕n. 名次；等級　rookie〔'rʊkɪ〕n. 新手

◇ top〔tɑp〕n.（棒球比賽的）上半局

◇ bottom〔'bɑtəm〕n.（棒球比賽的）下半局

◇ defense〔dɪ'fɛns〕v. 防守　　sacrifice fly 犧牲打

◇ go the distance 完全投球　　contest〔'kɑntɛst〕n. 比賽

◇ international game 國際賽

◇ open game 公開賽　　exhibition game 表演賽

- -

◇ cycling race 循環賽　　invitation game 邀請賽

◇ tournament game 錦標賽

◇ friendly competition 友誼賽　　elimination game 淘汰賽

◇ trial〔'traɪəl〕n.；a trial match；preliminary contest 預賽

◇ semifinal〔,sɛmə'faɪnl〕n. 準決賽（通常用複數 semifinals）

◇ final〔'faɪnl〕n. 決賽（常用複數 finals）

◇ champion〔'tʃæmpɪən〕n. 冠軍

- -

◇ runner-up〔'rʌnəˏʌp〕n. 亞軍

◇ ternary〔'tɜnɛrɪ〕n. 季軍　　rearward〔'rɪrwəd〕n. 殿軍

◇ even〔'ivən〕n. 平手；和局

◇ MVP（most valuable player）最優秀選手

◇ DH（designated hitter）代打

◇ RBI（runs batted in）得分

Movie

Costner shines in A Perfect World

Although *A Perfect World* is far from perfect, it succeeds in evoking compassion, empathy and pain.

A Perfect World is a moving film about a broken man, a trusting child and the impenetrable, special relationship that developed between them.

Butch Haynes (Kevin Costner) is a criminal who escapes from a Huntsville, Texas prison where he is serving 40 years for armed robbery. While on the run, he has taken eight-year old Phillip Perry (T.J. Lowther) hostage.

Costner delivers a powerful performance in the film, displaying the sensitivity and the depth needed to portray the complex man that Haynes is. He is convincing as a man whose mood swings shift from that of charming individual to a cold-blooded murderer.

For Costner fans, this is a must see. But even for those who are not, go see the movie and have a good cry. Maybe you'd start to like Costner.

解答 ☞ p. 265

1. How can the character of the criminal, Butch Haynes, best be described?
   (A) vicious
   (B) cold-blooded
   (C) highly changeable
   (D) superficial

2. What is the opinion expressed about the movie?
   (A) It is a perfect movie.
   (B) It is a terrible movie.
   (C) It manages to cause some strong feelings for the viewers.
   (D) It would be much worse without Costner.

3. What is *A Perfect World* about?
   (A) the complex relationship between a man and a young child
   (B) criminals in Texas
   (C) escape from a prison
   (D) an armed robbery

4. In conclusion, what does the paper say about the movie?
   (A) Only Costner fans will appreciate it.
   (B) It is a must see for everyone.
   (C) It is perfectly terrible.
   (D) Even non-Costner fans will appreciate the emotions of the movie.

科斯納在「強盜保鑣」綻放異彩

　　雖然「美好世界」（「強盜保鑣」之英文片名）一點也不美好，但卻成功地喚起人們的憐憫、共鳴與痛楚。

　　「強盜保鑣」這部感人肺腑的電影，是在描述一名失意的男子，一名容易輕信他人的小孩，以及在他們之間發展的那種無法理解的特殊關係。

　　布屈·海恩斯（凱文·科斯納飾），是一名從德州漢斯維爾監獄逃出的罪犯，他因為持械搶劫，在那裏坐了四十年的牢。在逃逸期間，他帶著八歲的非力普·伯瑞（T.J.羅瑟飾），作為人質。

　　凱文科斯納成功地詮釋了這名複雜男子個性的敏感和深沈。他扮演一位原本極具魅力的男子，最後卻成了一位冷血殺手。凱文科斯納的表現，非常具有說服力。

　　對於科斯納的影迷而言，這是部非看不可的影片。即使不是他的影迷，去看看這部電影，然後痛哭一場，也許你就會開始喜歡科斯納。

** evoke〔ɪ'vok〕v. 喚起　　compassion〔kəm'pæʃən〕n. 憐憫
　empathy〔'ɛmpəθɪ〕n. 共鳴　　trusting〔'trʌstɪŋ〕adj. 易相信他人的
　impenetrable〔ɪm'pɛnətrəbl〕adj. 不可理解的
　criminal〔'krɪmənl〕n. 罪犯　　armed〔ɑrmd〕adj. 武裝的
　robbery〔'rɑbərɪ〕n. 搶扨　　**on the run** 逃亡
　hostage〔'hɑstɪdʒ〕n. 人質　　display〔dɪ'sple〕v. 顯露；發揮
　sensitivity〔,sɛnsə'tɪvətɪ〕n. 敏感性；感受性
　portray〔por'tre〕v. 扮演　　complex〔'kɑmplɛks〕adj. 難懂的
　convincing〔kən'vɪnsɪŋ〕adj. 有說服力的
　swing〔swɪŋ〕v. 迴轉　　shift〔ʃɪft〕n. 改變

Concert

Sting to perform on Jan. 28-29

Sting will keep trysts with fans in Taiwan on Jan. 28 and 29 at the Taipei International Convention Center, announced Master Arts Promotion yesterday.

Taipei will be one of the stops in the Asian segment of the "Ten Summoner's Tales Tour." Sting will also perform in Japan, the Philippines, Australia, Indonesia, Malaysia and Singapore.

"Ten Summoner's Tales"—the title, drawn from Chaucer, is a pun on Sting's surname Sumner — is full of musical jokes and story-telling twists. According to a Reuter report, the record is a virtuoso exercise in playful craftsmanship after the darkness of his previous album, "The Soul Cages,"confronting the death of his father.

The 42-year-old British musician and actor said with a laugh during the interview with Reuter earlier this year: " I wanted to make it not autobiographical, essentially, not make it confessional. But given that that was my intention... I think I might have given away more by accident than by design."

解答☞ p. 265

1. Why is Sting's Tour called the "Ten Summoner's Tales Tour"?
   (A) There are ten songs.
   (B) The title sounds like his surname.
   (C) The title is decided on Summer.
   (D) The songs tell a lot of stories.

2. What was Sting's intention on this album?
   (A) He wanted to make it autobiographical.
   (B) He wanted to make it a tryst with his fans.
   (C) He didn't want it to be about himself, a confession.
   (D) He wanted to confront his father's death.

3. What is the " Ten Summoner's tales " like compared to his previous album of songs?
   (A) light   (B) dark
   (C) confrontational (D) an exercise

史汀將於一月廿八、廿九日來台演唱

開拓藝術推廣中心昨天宣布，史汀將遵守與歌迷的約定，於一月廿八、廿九日來台，在台北國際會議中心演唱。

台北是史汀 " Ten Summoner's Tales Tour " （專輯譯為「十個故事」）亞洲地區其中的一站。日本、菲律賓、澳大利亞、印尼、馬來西亞、新加坡等地，也在史汀的預定行程中。

" Ten Summoner's Tales " —— 這個標題是取材自英國文學家喬叟，同時也是史汀的姓 Sumner 的雙關語 —— 充滿了扭曲的音樂笑話與故事。根據路透社報導，史汀上一張專輯「靈魂枷鎖」發行期間，史汀的父親正好過世，渡過那段黑暗期之後，所推出的這張新專輯，運用了高度的詼諧技巧。

這位四十二歲的英籍音樂家兼演員，在年初與路透社記者訪談時，微笑地表示：

「我希望這張專輯唱片，在本質上不帶有自傳式或告白式的色彩。假定那是我的目標…我認為我把許多東西捨棄，是出於無心，而非有意。」

** tryst〔traɪst〕n. 約會　**keep tryst** 守約
announce〔ə'naʊns〕v. 宣布　segment〔'sɛgmənt〕n. 部份
pun〔pʌn〕n. 雙關語　surname〔'sɜ,nem〕n. 姓
twist〔twɪst〕n. 扭曲　virtuoso〔,vɜtʃʊ'oso〕n. 名家
playful〔'plefəl〕adj. 詼諧的
craftsmanship〔'kræftsmən,ʃɪp〕n. 技巧
album〔'ælbəm〕n. 專輯唱片　confront〔kən'frʌnt〕v. 面對；遭遇
autobiographical〔,ɔtə,baɪə'græfɪkl〕adj. 自傳式的
essentially〔ə'sɛnʃəlɪ〕adv. 本質上　**by accident** 偶然地

Basketball

Celtics extend winning streak to six

In Boston, Boston extended its season-best winning streak to six games, surviving a desperation comeback by Miami to win 103-98.

The Celtics led 99-87 before baskets by Glen Rice, Rony Seikaly and Matt Geiger made it 99-93 with 24 seconds left. Geiger's dunk made it 100-95 with 14 seconds remaining.

Warriors 108, Pistons 92

In Oakland, Calif., Latrell Sprewell scored 15 of his 27 points in the fourth quarter, helping Golden State hold off Detroit for its sixth consecutive home victory.

Lakers 103, Pacers 99

In Inglewood, Calif., Vlade Divac scored a season-high 26 points, including a three-point play with 1:03 left, carrying Los Angeles Lakers over Indiana.

76 ers 104, Mavericks 90

In Philadelphia, Dana Barros scored 22 points and Clarence Weatherspoon had 16 points and 10 rebounds as Philadelphia handed Dallas its 15th straight loss.

Associated Press

解答 ☞ p.265

1. Why were the Celtics on a season best winning streak?
   (A) They had won six games in a row— the best that season.
   (B) They had won six games unexpectedly.
   (C) They had won their first six games — their best season.
   (D) They had won six games at home.

2. What does a " desperation comeback " by Miami at the end suggest about the game before ?
   (A) It had been close all along.
   (B) Miami had lacked the will to win.
   (C) Miami had been leading until right at the end of the game.
   (D) The Celtics had been leading comfortably.

Focus

● 籃球相關字彙

basketball court 籃球場   jump ball 跳球
tackled ball 帶球   dribble〔'drɪbl〕 v. 運球
shooting 〔'ʃutɪŋ〕 n. 投籃
penalty shot 罰球   blocked shot "吃火鍋"

塞爾提克隊締造六連勝

波士頓塞爾提克隊在自家，成功地化解了邁阿密熱火隊的瘋狂反攻，以 103 比 98 獲勝，締造了六連勝的球季最佳戰績。

塞隊原本以 99 比 87 領先，但在對手葛雷·萊斯、羅尼·謝克利及馬特·蓋格三人聯手得分後，終場前 24 秒時，比數成了 99 比 93，僅剩 14 秒時，再加上蓋格的一記灌籃使比數成為 100 比 95。

勇士隊 108，活塞隊 92

在加州奧克蘭，史普瑞威爾在第四節得到他全場 27 分中的第 15 分，幫助金州勇士隊擊敗底特律活塞隊，保持了主場六連勝。

湖人隊 103，溜馬隊 99

在加州英格伍德，傅雷德·迪維克得到 26 分，為球季最高分，包括終場前一分零三秒的一記三分球，助洛杉磯湖人隊力克印地安那溜馬隊。

七六人隊 104，小牛隊 90

在費城，七六人隊的達那·巴羅斯得到 22 分，及克萊羅斯·威勒史普的 16 分、10 個籃板，使達拉斯小牛隊嚐到第 15 場連敗。

〔美聯社〕

** streak〔strik〕 n. 一連串
desperation〔,dɛspəˈreʃən〕 n. 不顧一切
comeback〔ˈkʌm,bæk〕 n. 反攻
basket〔ˈbæskɪt〕 n.（籃球的）得分
dunk〔dʌŋk〕 v. 浸 n. 灌籃　warrior〔ˈwɔrɪɚ,ˈwɑr-〕 n. 勇士；戰士
piston〔ˈpɪstn̩〕 n. 活塞　*hold off* 防備
consecutive〔kənˈsɛkjətɪv〕 adj. 連貫的
rebound〔rɪˈbaʊnd〕 n. 反彈；籃板球

Celebrity

Monday July 25

Whoopi Goldberg accused of ethnic stereotyping

Associated Press

New York — Actress Whoopi Goldberg was accused of ethnic stereotyping in a joke recipe she contributed to a Connecticut fund - raising cookbook.

Her "Jewish American Princess Fried Chicken" appears in "Cooking in Litchfield Hills," a cookbook sold to benefit the environmentalist Pratt Center. Goldberg has a house in affluent Litchfield County in northwestern Connecticut.

Among the recipe's directions : "Send a chauffeur to your favorite butcher shop for the chicken," "Watch your nails," and "Have cook prepare rest of meal while you touch up your makeup."

"I don't think it's funny," Abraham Foxman, national director of the Anti-Defamation League told the Daily News. "It's totally insensitive because it raises all the ugly anti-Semitic stereotypes."

Goldberg's publicist, Brad Cararelli, said : "Maybe (the critics) are not aware that Whoopi is Jewish, so she is certainly not anti-Semitic."

解答☞ p. 265

1. Whoopi Goldberg was accused of
   (A) criminal behavior.
   (B) irresponsible behavior.
   (C) being a racist.
   (D) being insensitive to another racial group.

2. What is the purpose of her book?
   (A) to give recipes to Jewish American Princesses
   (B) to help her as an actress
   (C) to benefit an environmental group
   (D) to make a joke

3. What do the recipe's directions suggest about Jewish American Princesses?
   (A) They are hard-working.
   (B) They are interested in cooking.
   (C) They are rich and lazy.
   (D) They are fond of fried chicken.

4. Why might Whoopi Goldberg not have been making Anti-Semitic remarks?
   (A) She is a sensitive person.
   (B) She was doing everything for an environmental group.
   (C) It was just a joke.
   (D) She is Jewish.

琥碧戈柏被指控有種族成見

〔美聯社〕女演員琥碧戈柏在為康乃狄克州籌募基金的一本食譜中，提供了一則好笑的配方，因而被指控具有種族成見。

她那則"猶太美籍公主炸雞"配方出現在"到里奇菲爾德山來做菜"這本食譜中。而銷售這本食譜是為了要替環保學家普瑞特·仙特籌措資金。琥碧戈柏本身，在康乃狄克州西北部的里奇菲爾德郡，擁有一棟不錯的房子。

在食譜的說明中，寫著：「叫司機到你最喜愛的肉店裏買雞肉」、「小心你的指甲」、以及「在你準備上妝之前，要厨師準備好其餘的餐點。」

反毀謗聯盟會的會長亞伯拉罕·福斯曼向每日新聞表示：「我看不出有什麼好笑的，這真是不顧別人的感覺，而且這則廣告可能會激起一些醜陋的、反猶太人的成見。」

琥碧戈柏的發言人布瑞德·卡拉瑞立表示：「也許那些批評家並不知道琥碧戈柏本身就是猶太人，所以她當然不會反猶太人。」

** accuse〔əˋkjuz〕v. 控告
ethnic〔ˋɛθnɪk〕adj. 人種的；民族（特有）的
recipe〔ˋrɛsəpɪ〕n. 食譜　　affluent〔ˋæflʋənt〕adj. 富裕的
county〔ˋkaʋntɪ〕n. 郡　　chauffeur〔ˋʃofɚ〕n. 司機
butcher〔ˋbʋtʃɚ〕n. 肉商
insensitive〔ɪnˋsɛnsətɪv〕adj. 不顧他人感受的
Semitic〔səˋmɪtɪk〕adj. 猶太人的
publicist〔ˋpʌblɪsɪst〕n. 發言人
Connecticut〔kəˋnɛtɪkət〕n. （美國）康乃狄克州
defamation〔ˌdɛfəˋmeʃən〕n. 中傷；破壞名譽

英文報紙必備影劇用語

◇ cinema〔'sɪnəmə〕n. ; movie theater 電影院

◇ grand opening 盛大獻映　　screen〔skrin〕n. 螢幕

◇ show time 放映時間　　　morning show 早場

◇ matinee〔,mætn'e〕n. 日場

◇ evening show 晚場　　late show 午夜場

◇ premiere〔prɪ'mɪr〕n. 首映　　rerun〔ri'rʌn〕n. 重播

◇ shatter all previous box office records 破票房記錄

◇ Dolby stereo 杜比超感立體音響

◇ literary film 文藝片　　comedy〔'kɑmədɪ〕n. 喜劇

◇ tragedy〔'trædʒədɪ〕n. 悲劇　　thriller 驚悚片

◇ detective film 偵探片　　kung-fu film 動作片

◇ swordsmen film 武俠片　　horror film 恐怖片

◇ musical〔'mjuzɪkḷ〕n. 歌舞劇；音樂片

◇ science film 科幻片

◇ director〔də'rɛktɚ,daɪ-〕n. 導演

◇ producer〔prə'djusɚ〕n. 製片

◇ cameraman〔'kæmərə,mæn〕n. 攝影師

◇ actor〔'æktɚ〕n. 男演員　　actress〔'æktrɪs〕n. 女演員

◇ Academy Awards 影藝學院金像獎

◇ Oscar Awards 奧斯卡金像獎

◇ Venice International Movie Festival 維尼斯國際影展

◊ Cannes International Movie Festival 坎城國際影展
◊ Berlin International Movie Festival 柏林國際影展
◊ Asian Movie Festival 亞洲影展
◊ Golden Horse Film Festival 金馬獎影展
◊ Golden Horse Prize 金馬獎

◊ pop music 流行樂　　rock n' roll 搖滾樂
◊ hit music 熱門樂　　mass communication 大眾傳播
◊ channel〔'tʃænḷ〕n. 頻道
◊ FM（frequency modulation）調頻
◊ AM（amplitude modulation）調幅
◊ variety show 綜藝節目　　interview show 訪問節目

◊ quiz show 猜謎節目　　soap opera 連續劇
◊ children's show 兒童節目　　news & weather 新聞氣象
◊ program director 導播　　teleplay〔'tɛlɪˌple〕n. 電視劇
◊ commercial〔kə'mɝʃəl〕n.（電視、廣播的）商業廣告
◊ promotional trailer 節目預告
◊ Emmy Award 艾美獎　　Golden Bell Award 金鐘獎

Figure skating

Harding 'virtually certain' to face criminal charge

PORTLAND, Ore.— Tonya Harding, whose ex-husband reportedly is prepared to testify she was involved in the plot to disable figure skating rival Nancy Kerrigan, is "virtually certain " to face criminal charges, The Oregonian newspaper reported in Wednesday's editions.

Sources told the newspaper that Harding's former husband, Jeff Gillooly, was willing to admit his own role in the attack on Nancy Kerrigan and testify that Harding helped plan the assault as well as cover it up after learning the FBI was investigating.

The report came on the heels of a television report Tuesday night that Gillooly, charged with conspiracy to assault Kerrigan, hopes to have a plea bargain worked out by the end of the week that implicates Harding.

Associated Press

解答 ☞ p. 265

1. Will Harding face charges for the attempt to disfigure her rival?
   (A) perhaps
   (B) probably
   (C) unlikely
   (D) almost definitely

2. What is Harding's ex-husband willing to testify to?
   (A) his innocence and Harding's guilt
   (B) his innocence and Harding's innocence
   (C) that everything was planned by Harding
   (D) his guilt and Harding's guilt

3. A plea bargain is
   (A) an admission of guilt.
   (B) proof of innocence.
   (C) information in return for lighter punishment.
   (D) asking the judge for mercy.

FOCUS

● 溜冰相關字彙
   rink〔rɪŋk〕*n.* 溜冰場　edge〔ɛdʒ〕*n.* 冰刀
   roller skater 輪式溜冰鞋
   figure skating 花式溜冰
   roller skating 輪式溜冰
   telemark〔'tɛlə,mɑrk〕*n.* 屈膝旋轉
   levee jump 飛跳

哈汀極有可能被起訴

波特蘭，奧瑞岡電——據「奧瑞岡人報」星期三的報導指出，湯妮雅‧哈汀的前夫準備出庭作證，指證她涉嫌傷害罪，有意讓同為花式滑冰選手的南茜‧凱麗根無法參加選拔。因此，我們「幾乎可以確定」她將面臨起訴。

消息來源告知該報，哈汀的前夫傑夫‧葛洛里願意坦承他曾參與攻擊南茜‧凱麗根，並指證哈汀曾協助策劃此次攻擊，並且，在得知聯邦調查局開始進行調查後，哈汀掩飾其犯罪行為。

上述報導是緊隨在週二晚間一則電視報導後傳出的。此報導指出被控涉嫌攻擊凱麗根的葛洛里希望在本週內與檢方達成交易，以換取從輕量刑的條件。〔美聯社〕

** virtually〔'vɝtʃʊəlɪ〕adv. 幾乎　　criminal〔'krɪmənḷ〕adj. 犯罪的
charge〔tʃɑrdʒ〕n. 控告　　ex-husband〔ˌɛks'hʌzbənd〕n. 前夫
testify〔'tɛstə,faɪ〕v. 作證　　plot〔plɑt〕n. 陰謀
disable〔dɪs'ebḷ〕v. 使～失去資格　　**figure skating** 花式滑冰
rival〔'raɪvḷ〕n. 對手　　assault〔ə'tlɔc〕n. 攻擊
investigate〔ɪn'vɛstə,get〕v. 調查　　**on the heel of** 緊接而來
conspiracy〔kən'spɪrəsɪ〕n. 共謀　　plea〔pli〕n. 懇求
bargain〔'bɑrgɪn〕n. 交易　　implicate〔'ɪmplɪ,ket〕v. 與～有牽連

Band

Beatles reunion likely on TV

The Beatles may reunite. But they'll only let it be on TV. Former Beatle Paul Mc-Cartney says the three surviving members of the group could perform together again, but only in a documentary being prepared by British television.

McCartney says he started playing old Beatles tunes after he realized that other bands were having success with them. " I discovered that they (the songs) are still fresh and interesting. It was like learning them all over again," he said in a conference before the first of two concerts in Italy.

No date has been set for the release of the Beatle documentary.

解答 ☞ p. 265

1. What did Paul McCartney say about the Beatles?
   (A) They would reunite to form the old group.
   (B) They could reunite to play for a television program.
   (C) They would only be interviewed together, not play.
   (D) Sometimes the three surviving members play together, but it's not the Beatles.

2. Paul McCartney discovered
   (A) that songs he had helped write are still interesting to play.
   (B) that people were making a lot of money out of his songs.
   (C) that he could make a lot of money out of his old songs.
   (D) that he could play the old Beatles' songs with the surviving members of the group.

披頭士可能在電視上重聚

　　披頭士合唱團可能復團，但只有在電視上出現。前披頭士團員保羅・麥卡尼表示，三名在世的團員可能會再聚在一起表演，但只會在由英國電視台製作的一部記錄片中出現。

　　麥卡尼表示，在得知其他合唱團演唱披頭士的歌曲成功之後，他開始彈奏這些老歌，他在義大利二場演唱會的第一場前的記者會中表示：「我發現他們（指歌曲）仍舊新鮮有趣，就像我重新學這些歌一樣。」

　　至於披頭士記錄片播放的日期則尚未決定。

＊＊ reunion〔ri'junjən〕*n.* 重聚　　reunite〔,rijʊ'naɪt〕*v.* 再結合
survive〔sə'vaɪv〕*v.* 還存在
documentary〔,dɑkjə'mɛntərɪ〕*n.* 記錄片
tune〔tjun〕*n.* 曲調　　band〔bænd〕*n.* 樂團
conference〔'kɑnfərəns〕*n.* 會議
concert〔'kɑnsɝt〕*n.* 演唱會　　release〔rɪ'lis〕*v.* 發行；放映

Thursday Oct. 27

Pepsi-Michael Jackson marriage fizzles

Associated Press

New York — Michael Jackson and Pepsico are parting ways.

The soft drink giant canned its backing of the superstar on Sunday, two days after Jackson backed out of a world tour claiming he was addicted to painkillers.

His habit took hold after he was burned by a fire on a Pepsi commercial set in 1984, Jackson said.

The Pepsi endorsement was scheduled to end at the same time that Jackson's " Dangerous " tour ended. Jackson called a halt to the tour Friday.

" The cancellation of the tour really effectively cancels our relationship with Michael right now, " Pepsi spokesman Gary Hemphill said Saturday. " We just hope he is able to resolve his problems. "

解答☞ p. 265

1. When did Pepsi stop its backing of Michael Jackson?
   (A) after the end of the Dangerous Tour
   (B) after he became addicted to painkillers
   (C) two days after he cancelled his world tour
   (D) after Jackson was canned

2. Why did Jackson take painkillers?
   (A) the pressure of the world tour
   (B) because of continuing medical problems
   (C) because of back problems
   (D) because he had become addicted to them

3. What was Pepsi's response to the problems?
   (A) They cancelled their relationship with Jackson and
       condemned him.
   (B) They tried to resolve his drug problem and restart
       the tour.
   (C) They cancelled their relationship with him but wished
       him well.
   (D) They consulted their attorney about possible legal
       action.

麥克傑克森與百事公司拆夥

〔美聯社〕紐約電——麥可傑克森和百事可樂分道揚鑣了。

自傑克森聲稱他服用止痛藥上癮，而從世界巡迴演唱中打退堂鼓，兩天之後，也就是在週日，這家飲料界巨人撤消了對這位超級巨星的支持。

傑克森表示，自從他在一九八四年，百事可樂的廣告中，被火燒傷後，便養成了服止痛藥的習慣。

百事公司計劃在「危險」之旅演唱會結束後，停止對傑克森的贊助。傑克森的危險之旅行程已叫停。

百事公司發言人蓋瑞・漢姆菲爾於週六表示，危險之旅的取消，我們和麥可的合作關係，亦立即解除。」「我們只希望他能夠解決他的問題。」

** fizzle〔ˈfɪzl̩〕v.（計劃等）夭折　　can〔kæn〕v. 停止
claim〔klem〕v. 聲稱　　addicted〔əˈdɪktɪd〕adj. 耽溺於
painkiller〔ˈpenˌkɪlə〕n. 止痛藥　　***take hold*** 固定；落實
commercial〔kəˈmɚʃəl〕n. 商業廣告
endorsement〔ɪnˈdɔrsmənt〕n. 贊助
schedule〔ˈskɛdʒʊl〕v. 預定
cancellation〔ˌkænsəˈleʃəl〕n. 取消

Oscar

'Schindler's List' sweeps Oscars

By Matt Spetalnick
Reuter

Los Angeles, March 21 — Steven Spielberg, who has created Hollywood's biggest box office hits only to be snubbed every year on Oscar night, finally broke his legendary jinx Monday night as his Holocaust epic " Schindler's List " swept the Academy Awards.

Tom Hanks picked up the Best Actor award for his portrayal of a lawyer with AIDS in " Philadelphia,"and Holly Hunter was named Best Actress for her role in "The Piano " as a mute Scottish mail-order bride.

解答 ☞ p. 265

1. Who won the Best Actor award ?
   (A) Schindler   (B) Steven Spielberg
   (C) Tom Hanks   (D) Holly Hunter

2. Steven Spielberg
   (A) is always the biggest winner in the Academy Awards.
   (B) has created Hollywood's biggest box office hits.
   (C) directs " The Piano ".
   (D) portrays a lawyer with AIDS in "Philadelphia".

「辛德勒的名單」縱橫奧斯卡

〔路透社〕洛杉磯，三月廿一日電—— 史蒂芬‧史匹柏，這位總是創造好萊塢最高票房的導演，以往總在奧斯卡晚會中被冷落。週一晚上，他終於得以翻身，以一部敍述德國人屠殺猶太人的史詩鉅片「辛德勒的名單」，成為本屆奧斯卡獎最大贏家。

湯姆漢克斯在「費城」一片中，飾演一名患有愛滋病的律師，而獲得最佳男主角。最佳女主角由荷莉韓特獲得，她在「鋼琴師和她的情人」一片中，飾演一位漂洋過海的蘇格蘭啞巴新娘。

** ***box office*** 票房　　hit〔hɪt〕*n.* 叫好又叫座的電影
snub〔snʌb〕*v.* 冷落　　legendary〔'lɛdʒəndˌɛrɪ〕*n.* 傳說的
jinx〔dʒɪŋks〕*n.* 不吉利的事物　　holocaust〔'halə,kɔst〕*n.* 大屠殺
the Holocaust （納粹黨的）猶太人大屠殺
epic〔'ɛpɪk〕*n.* 史詩　　academy〔ə'kædəmɪ〕*n.* 學院
pick up 得到　　portrayal〔por'treəl〕*n.* 描寫
Philadelphia〔ˌfɪlə'dɛlfjə, -fɪə〕*n.* 費城
mute〔mjut〕*adj.* 啞的；不能說話的
Scottish〔'skɑtɪʃ〕*adj.* 蘇格蘭的；蘇格蘭人（語）的
mail-order〔'mel'ɔdɚ〕*adj.* 郵購的

Star Taylor operated

Reuter/Associated Pressr

Los Angeles, March 24— Actress Elizabeth Taylor underwent hip replacement surgery as planned and the operation went smoothly, her doctor said Thursday.

"There were no surgical complications." Doctor John Moreland said in a statement issued the day after surgery.

The 62-year-old Oscar-winning actress underwent the operation after specialists diagnosed her with osteoarthritis of the left hip, a condition in which vital cartilage has worn out.

解答 ☞ p. 265

1. Why was the operation done on Elizabeth Taylor?
   (A) to repair her
   (B) to relieve hip pain
   (C) to reduce pressure on the hip
   (D) to replace her hip artificially

2. What was the doctor's comment on the operation?
   (A) It was a simple operation.
   (B) It is frequently dangerous.
   (C) The surgeons encountered no problems.
   (D) They will have to wait a few days after surgery to see.

3. What was the problem with Taylor's hip?
   (A) Cartilage in the hip joint had worn out.
   (B) There was a vital problem in her left hip joint.
   (C) She had a special form of osteoarthritis.
   (D) She needed a diagnosis of her hip.

FOCUS

Elizabeth Taylor 在連續四年獲奧斯卡提名後，終於在 1960 年以 Butterfield 8 (青樓艷妓) 獲得奧斯卡金像獎。其間遭受了丈夫死亡、再婚及肺炎折磨，真可謂之苦盡甘來。

玉婆手術順利

〔路透社／美聯社〕洛杉磯，三月廿四日電——女星伊莉莎白·泰勒的醫生週四表示，玉婆的臀部移植手術按照計劃進行，一切順利。

約翰·莫蘭德在手術後的聲明中指出：「並沒有併發症。」

這位年屆六十二歲的奧斯卡影后動了此次手術，原因是專家診斷她的左臀患了關節炎，有塊重要的軟骨已經磨壞了。

** hip〔hɪp〕*n.* 臀部
replacement〔rɪˈplesmənt〕*n.* 替換
surgery〔ˈsɜdʒərɪ〕*n.* （外科）手術
surgical〔ˈsɜdʒɪkl〕*adj.* 外科的
complication〔ˌkɑmpləˈkeʃən〕*n.* 併發症
undergo〔ˌʌndəˈgo〕*v.* 遭受
specialist〔ˈspɛʃəlɪst〕*n.* 專家
diagnose〔ˌdaɪəgˈnos, -ˈnoz〕*v.* 診斷
osteoarthritis〔ˌɑstɪoɑrˈθraɪtɪs〕*n.* 骨關節炎
vital〔ˈvaɪtl̩〕*adj.* 極重要的
cartilage〔ˈkɑrtl̩ɪdʒ〕*n.* 軟骨
wear out 磨壞

Part 5

Life & Medicine 生活醫藥

Environment   *Wednesday Mar. 16*

How bad is battery pollution?

Electronic-gadget-loving Americans buy 2.5 billion batteries a year and throw away more than 90 percent of them. These disposable batteries contain toxic materials such as mercury.

Because of battery-collection problems, very few are recycled. Instead, their harmful contents may leak from landfills or — more likely — fall to the ground from incinerator stacks.

Remedies are generating both positive and negative results. Most new single-use batteries are designed to work with little or no mercury. Button cells, often powering watches and cameras, are increasingly being made with silver oxide or lithium. Batteries that can be recharged 300 to 1,000 times have reduced landfill waste. But most are nickel-cadmium rechargeables. When eventually discarded, they put hundreds of tons of highly toxic cadmium a year into the environment.

解答☞ p. 266

1. The most probable way for battery contents to pollute is
   (A) during the recycling process.
   (B) because of problems of collecting batteries.
   (C) when they leak from landfills.
   (D) during the incineration process.

2. New designs for single-use batteries try to
   (A) avoid recycling problems.
   (B) generate both positive and negative electricity.
   (C) work with materials which don't leak.
   (D) avoid using mercury.

FOCUS

●環保相關字彙

ozone layer 臭氧層　public hearing 公開聽證會
leakage〔'likɪdʒ〕n. 洩漏物
lethal〔'liθəl〕adj. 致命的
extinction〔ɪk'stɪŋkʃən〕n. 滅亡；滅絕
conservation〔,kɑnsɚ'veʃən〕n. 保存
disfigure〔dɪs'fɪgjɚ〕v. 破壞；損毀

電池污染有多嚴重？

愛好電子機械用品的美國人一年要買二十五億個電池，其中有百分之九十以上會被丟棄。這些用完即丟的電池，含有如汞之類的有毒物質。

由於回收電池困難重重，因此很少能再生製造。然而，那些有害的物質可能會從垃圾掩埋場滲出，或更可能從焚化爐架滲入泥土中。

補救的方法會造成正面及負面的結果。多數新製的只能用一次的電池，在設計上儘量避免使用汞，或甚至完全不用。手錶或相機上的袖珍扣形電池，逐漸改爲以氧化銀或鋰製成。可以充電三百至一千次的電池，使得掩埋場中的廢棄物減少。但是他們大多是含鎳及鎘的可充電電池。被丟棄之後，每年會釋放出幾百噸高毒性的鎘於環境中。

** battery〔'bætərɪ〕n. 電池　　gadget〔'gædʒɪt〕n. (小的)機械
disposable〔dɪ'spozəbl̩〕adj. 用完即丟的
toxic〔'taksɪk〕adj. 有毒的　mercury〔'mɝkjərɪ〕n. 水銀
recycle〔ri'saɪkl̩〕v. 再生利用　　content〔'kantɛnt〕n. 含量
leak〔lik〕v. 漏出　　　landfill〔'lænd, fɪl〕n. 掩埋場
incinerator〔ɪn'sɪnə, retɚ〕n. 焚化爐　　stack〔stæk〕n. 架子
remedy〔'rɛmədɪ〕n. 改善方法　positive〔'pazətɪv〕adj. 正面的
negative〔'nɛgətɪv〕adj. 負面的　oxide〔'aksaɪd〕n. 氧化物
lithium〔'lɪθɪəm〕n. 鋰　　recharge〔ri'tʃɑrdʒ〕v. 再充電
nickel‑cadmium〔'nɪkl̩'kædmɪəm〕adj. 含鎳及鎘的
discard〔dɪs'kɑrd〕v. 丟棄

Earthquake

Heavy losses possible without "The Big One"

PASADENA— The earthquake that struck California on Monday wasn't the Big One. And that's the problem.

The quake was believed to have done nothing to ease pressure on the dreaded San Andreas Fault. That's where the Big One would occur, possibly causing cataclysmic damage and widespread death and injury.

Scientists said the quake was caused by the constant movement of Southern California toward San Francisco, which places enormous stress on the Los Angeles Basin.

The Richter scale is a measure of ground motion as recorded on seismographs. Every increase of one number means a tenfold increase in magnitude. Thus a reading of 7.5 reflects an earthquake 10 times stronger than one of 6.5.

Scientists said Monday's quake showed that timing and location can be just as important as magnitude—and that Southern California doesn't need a Big One to suffer heavy losses.

解答☞p.266

1. What was the problem of Monday's earthquake?
   (A) It wasn't the Big One.
   (B) It was a 6.6 on the Richter scale.
   (C) It showed that even smaller earthquakes can cause much damage.
   (D) It showed that an even bigger earthquake would hit within 30 years.

2. According to scientists, the earthquake was caused by
   (A) the San Andreas Fault.
   (B) pressure due to the movement of Southern California towards San Francisco.
   (C) the pressure of moving to San Francisco from the Los Angeles Basin.
   (D) the enormous stress of Los Angeles.

3. An earthquake five times stronger than a 6.6 quake would measure
   (A) 8.0 on the Richter scale.
   (B) 33.0 on the Richter scale.
   (C) 7.6 on the Richter scale.
   (D) 7.1 on the Richter scale.

地震不大，也可能損失慘重

巴沙地那電——星期一襲擊加州的地震規模並不大，但這正是問題所在。

一般相信此次地震並未減弱可怕的聖安德瑞斯斷層中之壓力，而此地卻是大地震最可能爆發之處，它可能會造成災難性的損失及廣泛的傷亡。

科學家說此次地震是因為南加州板塊不斷地移向舊金山板塊，使洛杉磯盆地承受巨大壓力。

芮氏地震標準是測量地震儀上所顯示的地質運動。每增加一級，地震強度即增強十倍。因此，七點五級的地震強度要比六點五級大上十倍。

科學家表示，星期一的地震顯示，地震發生的時間和位置，與強度一樣重要——也就是說，南加州不一定要受到大地震侵襲才會損失慘重。

** San Andreas Fault 聖安德瑞斯斷層
cataclysmic〔͵kætə'klɪzmɪk〕*adj.* 災難性的
constant〔'kɑnstənt〕*adj.* 不斷的
enormous〔ɪ'nɔrməs〕*adj.* 巨大的   stress〔strɛs〕*n.* 壓力
the Los Angeles Basin 洛杉磯盆地
Richter scale 芮氏地震分等標準
seismograph〔'saɪzmə͵græf〕*n.* 地震計
tenfold〔'tɛn'fold〕*adj.* 十倍的
magnitude〔'mægnə͵tjud〕*n.* 強度

Adults watch TV, skip exercise

By Lauran Neergaard
Associated Press

Washington—Americans know they need to exercise more for good health. But a new survey shows they have no intention of doing it.

Sixty-four percent of those polled said they would like to exercise more because they know it's healthy, but say they can't find the time. They said they had fewer than 10 hours of leisure time every week.

But 84 percent watch television at least three hours a week, meaning they have time for physical activity but are too lazy or prefer television, the survey concluded. And 41 percent said they weren't likely to improve anytime soon.

Regular exercise lowers cholesterol and blood pressure and helps thwart heart disease and other illnesses. Nobody knows how much disease a sedentary lifestyle actually causes, but the Atlanta-based Centers for Dissease Control and Prevention estimates that the nation spends US$5.7 billion annually in medical care and lost productivity for sedentary people with heart disease alone.

解答 ☞ p.266

1. Most Americans :
   (A) are aware of the benefits of regular exercise, but don't like doing it.
   (B) are only partly aware of the benefits of regular exercise but avoid doing it.
   (C) are aware of the benefits of regular exercise, but claim they can't find the time.
   (D) are aware of the benefits of regular exercise, but after work and leisure there is no time.

2. The survey concluded :
   (A) A majority of Americans were unable to do exercise because of a lack of time.
   (B) A majority of Americans did have the time to exercise, but only a minority intended to improve their exercise situation.
   (C) Most Americans would rather watch television than improve their health.
   (D) Most Americans have the time to exercise, but are either too lazy, or would rather watch television, and a large minority wasn't likely to improve soon.

3. What is the effect of regular exercise on disease ?
   (A) It helps prevent heart and other diseases and lowers cholesterol and blood pressure levels.
   (B) Nobody really knows its real effect on disease.
   (C) It is lowered when cholesterol and blood pressure thwart heart disease.
   (D) It is restricted to lowering cholesterol and blood-pressure, the causes of heart disease.

成年人只顧看電視而忘了運動

〔美聯社〕華盛頓電——美國人知道他們必須多做運動來保持健康。但一項新的調查顯示，他們根本不想做運動。

在民意調查中，有百分之六十四的人們表示想多做運動，因為他們知道運動有益健康，但卻沒有時間做。他們表示一星期中，空閒時間不及十小時。

但此項調查的結論指出，有百分之八十四的人，一星期至少看三小時電視，這意謂著他們有時間做運動，卻太懶惰或比較喜歡看電視。而且，有百分之四十一的人表示，在短期內，他們可能不會做任何改變。

定期運動可降低膽固醇及高血壓，而且能防止心臟及其他疾病。沒人知道長期坐著的習慣會眞正引起多少疾病，但是，亞特蘭大疾病控制和預防中心估計，爲了患有心臟疾病又習慣坐著的人，國家每年要花費五十七億美金的醫療費用，而且國民生產力也因此降低。

** skip〔skɪp〕v. 忽略　　　survey〔'sɝve〕n. 調查
regular〔'rɛgjələ〕adj. 定期的
cholesterol〔kə'lɛstə,rol〕n. 膽固醇　　thwart〔θwɔrt〕v. 阻礙
sedentary〔'sɛdn̩,tɛrɪ〕adj. 常坐著的
estimate〔'ɛstə,met〕v. 估計
productivity〔,prodʌk'tɪvətɪ〕n. 生產力

Health

Monday Nov. 21

Doctors say alcohol good for the heart

Reuter

Atlanta, Nov. 9 — Moderate alcohol consumption appears to lower heart attack risk, but a group of doctors said Tuesday they weren't ready to prescribe alcohol for non-drinkers with heart disease.

"Small amounts of alcohol with meals is a part of a healthy lifestyle," said Dr. Curtis Ellison, professor of medicine at Boston University. "The data support that very strongly."

Nevertheless, Dr. Arthur Klatsky of Kaiser Permanente Medical Center in Oakland, California, who studied the drinking habits and heart problems of 2,015 people, said, "Non-drinkers are best left alone."

On the other hand, Ellison said, it would be a mistake to counsel light drinkers to give up drinking altogether as a way of reducing heart risk.

解答 ☞ p. 266

1. Moderate alcohol consumption :
   (A) should not be prescribed to people as it risks a heart attack.
   (B) should not be prescribed to drinkers with heart disease.
   (C) could usefully be prescribed to drinkers with heart disease.
   (D) might be proved to be useful to people with heart disease, but doctors are not yet ready to prescribe it.

2. The data support the assertion that :
   (A) alcohol can only be useful if taken with meals.
   (B) alcohol in limited amounts contributes to a healthy lifestyle.
   (C) alcohol is only a small part of a healthy lifestyle.
   (D) moderation in all things, especially alcohol, is important to a healthy lifestyle.

3. Having studied drinking habits and heart problems, Dr. Klatsky said :
   (A) Non-drinkers do not need medical help for heart problems.
   (B) Non-drinkers should not be made to drink in hospital.
   (C) Non-drinkers should be told not to drink for heart problems.
   (D) Doctors should not make recommendations about alcohol to non-drinkers.

醫生表示酒對心臟有益

〔路透社〕亞特蘭大，十一月九日電——適度的飲酒似乎能夠降低得心臟病的危險，但一群醫生週二表示，對於不喝酒的人，他們不準備以酒來治療其心臟疾病。

波士頓大學醫學教授艾力生博士表示：「用餐時喝少量的酒，是健康生活方式的一部分。」「有數據足以證明。」

然而，加州奧克蘭的凱瑟·培門內特醫學中心的克萊斯基博士，曾針對二千零一十五名人士的飲酒習慣和心臟問題做過研究，他表示：「不喝酒的人最好別接受這項治療方式。」

艾力生表示，另一方面，如果勸告那些只淺酌的人完全不喝酒，以減少心臟病的危險，這是錯誤的。

** alcohol 〔'ælkə,hɔl〕 n. 酒
moderate 〔'madərɪt〕 adj. 適度的
consumption 〔,kən'sʌmpʃən〕 n. 消耗
prescribe 〔prɪ'skraɪb〕 v. 開藥方　　*leave alone* 別干涉
counsel 〔'kaunsḷ〕 v. 勸告

英文報紙必備醫藥用語

◇ fitness center 衞生所　　general hospital 綜合醫院

◇ polyclinic〔ˌpɑlɪ'klɪnɪk〕n. 綜合診所

◇ sanatorium〔ˌsænə'torɪəm〕n. 療養院

◇ register〔'rɛdʒɪstɚ〕v. 掛號　diagnostic charge 診療費

◇ out-patient service 門診　　emergency call 急診

◇ ward〔wɔrd〕n. 病房　　patient〔'peʃənt〕n. 病人

◇ hospitalization〔ˌhɑspɪtəlɪ'zeʃən〕n. 住院

◇ discharge patient 出院　　general medicine 一般內科

◇ G. I. 腸胃科　　dermatology〔ˌdɝmə'tɑlədʒɪ〕n. 皮膚科

◇ urology〔jʊ'rɑlədʒɪ〕n. 泌尿科

◇ ophthalmology〔ˌɑfθæl'mɑlədʒɪ〕n. 眼科

◇ otolaryngology〔ˌotəˌlærɪŋ'gɑlədʒɪ〕n. 耳鼻喉科

◇ dentistry〔'dɛntɪstrɪ〕n. 牙科　　ethics of medicine 醫德

◇ complication〔ˌkɑmplə'keʃən〕n. 併發症

◇ deterioration〔dɪˌtɪrɪə'reʃən〕n. 惡化

◇ malnutrition〔ˌmælnju'trɪʃən〕n. 營養不良

◇ throw up; vomit〔'vɑmɪt〕v. 嘔吐

◇ mental stress 精神緊張　　trauma〔'traʊmə〕n. 外傷

◇ inflame〔ɪn'flem〕v. 發炎　　food poisoning 食物中毒

◇ unconscious〔ʌn'kɑnʃəs〕adj. 無意識的

◇ prescribe〔prɪ'skraɪb〕v. 開藥方

◇ formula〔'fɔrmjələ〕*n*. 藥方

◇ dosage〔'dosɪdʒ〕*n*. 藥量；劑量

◇ dose〔dos〕*n*. 一劑　　blood type 血型

◇ anemia〔ə'nimɪə〕*n*. 貧血　　bleeding〔'blidɪŋ〕*n*. 出血

◇ artificial respiration 人工呼吸

◇ nothing by mouth 禁食　　heat stroke 中暑

◇ homosexuality〔,homə,sɛkʃʊ'ælətɪ〕*n*. 同性戀

◇ hard of hearing 重聽　　decayed tooth 蛀牙

◇ nearsightedness〔'nɪr'saɪtɪd,nɪs〕*n*. 近視

◇ rhinitis〔raɪ'naɪtɪs〕*n*. 鼻炎

◇ influenza〔,ɪnflʊ'ɛnzə〕*n*. 流行性感冒 (亦作 flu)

◇ infectious disease 傳染病

◇ arthritis〔ɑr'θraɪtɪs〕*n*. 關節炎

◇ rheumatism〔'rumə,tɪzəm〕*n*. 風濕症

◇ diabetes〔,daɪə'bitɪs〕*n*. 糖尿病

◇ abortion〔ə'bɔrʃən〕*n*. 墮胎　　vein〔ven〕*n*. 靜脈

◇ surgery〔'sɝdʒɪrɪ〕*n*. 外科手術　　hot compress 熱敷

◇ sterilize〔'stɛrə,laɪz〕*v*. 消毒

◇ dissection〔dɪ'sɛkʃən〕*n*. 解剖　　height〔haɪt〕*n*. 身高

◇ BP (blood pressure) 血壓　　weight〔wet〕*n*. 體重

◇ health examination 健康檢查

◇ artery〔'ɑrtərɪ〕*n*. 動脈　　surrogate mother 代理孕母

◇ sterility〔stə'rɪlətɪ〕*n*. 不孕症

Saturday Dec. 14

Smiles can get rid of stress: safety council

Reuter

London, Dec.13 — Put a smile on your face and you can prolong life by reducing stress, the British Safety Council says.

The council launched a Smile for Safety Week with a call for people to grin their way to a healthier lifestyle.

"Smiling is the key to wellness and now is the time to start on the road to a happier, healthier, stress-free life," said the council's director general James Tye.

Tye said it was particularly important to put on a cheery face in the run-up to the Christmas period, traditionally the most stressful time of the year.

The council said stress-related disorders affected an estimated third of Britain's workforce, resulting in the loss of 90 million working days a year at a cost of seven billion pounds sterling (US$10.50 billion).

The disorders included ulcers, headaches, backaches, high blood pressure, mental problems, tiredness and asthma.

解答☞ p. 266

1. According to the British Safety Council, which statement is true?
   (A) All you have to do is smile and you will live longer.
   (B) Smiling reduces stress and can thereby prolong life.
   (C) Reducing stress is the reason you should smile.
   (D) People in Britain aren't healthy because they aren't happy enough with their lives.

2. The council launched a campaign
   (A) to promote grinning.
   (B) to promote a healthier lifestyle through smiling.
   (C) to promote longevity.
   (D) to promote feeling good and looking younger.

3. The council's director general said that it was important to put on a cheery face at Christmas because
   (A) stress is a Christmas tradition.
   (B) Christmas is a time to be happy.
   (C) the period just before Christmas is very stressful.
   (D) Christmas should not be stressful.

FOCUS

● 微笑相關字彙
   smile〔smaɪl〕v. 微笑
   chuckle〔'tʃʌkl〕v. 低聲地笑
   grin〔grɪn〕v. 露齒而笑
   giggle〔'gɪgl〕v. 吃吃地笑
   guffaw〔gʌ'fɔ〕v. 高聲笑　sneer〔snɪr〕v. 冷笑

微笑能消除緊張

〔路透社〕倫敦，十二月十三日電——英國安全會議指出，臉上掛著笑容能讓你藉著消除緊張而延年益壽。

在這次的會議中，將著手籌畫一項微笑安全週的活動，號召人們以微笑迎向更健康的生活方式。

會議的指導會長詹姆士‧泰說：「微笑是健康之鑰，而且現在是展開更歡樂、更健康、沒有壓力的生活路程的時刻。」

泰並且說，在聖誕節籌備期間，是傳統上一年中最繁忙的時刻，一張愉悅的臉尤其重要。

會議並談到與壓力相關的一些病痛，影響了英國大約三分之一的工作人數，造成一年九億個工作天的損失，相當於一年七十億英鎊（美金一百零五億）的代價。

這些病痛包括潰瘍、頭痛、背痛、高血壓、精神問題、疲倦與氣喘。

** longevity〔lɑn'dʒɛvətɪ〕n. 長壽　　council〔'kaʊnsl̩〕n. 會議
launch〔lɔntʃ〕v. 開始　　　　grin〔grɪn〕v. 露齒而笑
director〔də'rɛktɚ〕n. 董事；指導者
general〔'dʒɛnərəl〕n. 會長；將軍　run-up〔'rʌn,ʌp〕n. 籌備期間
estimate〔'ɛstə,met〕v. 估計
workforce〔'wɜk,fɔrs〕n. 勞工總人數
sterling〔'stɜlɪŋ〕n. 英國貨幣　　　ulcer〔'ʌlsɚ〕n. 潰瘍
asthma〔'æzmə,'æsmə〕n. 氣喘

Environment

ROC a dumping site for toxic waste: Greenpeace

Compiled by
The China Post

Taiwan is fast becoming a dumping site of toxic waste for industrialized countries, warns Greenpeace, the international environmental protection organization.

Greenpeace wrote to the ROC's Environmental Protection Administration on March 11, noting that Taiwan has imported over 2000 tons of toxic waste from the U.S. and Britain during the first six months of 1992 alone, the Independence Evening Post reported yesterday.

According to a Greenpeace study, goods "recycled" in the U.S. are not actually recycled there but instead the recyclable wastes are shipped to countries such as Taiwan, South Korea, Pakistan, mainland China and the Philippines.

The ROC's environmental protection laws only bar imports of toxic substances but allow imports of plastics and other materials which become toxic after burning.

The huge influx of foreign waste to Taiwan has reduced the price of domestic garbage, making producers and consumers in the island less willing to recycle their waste because of the narrow profit margin, the local press asserted.

解答☞ p. 266

1. According to Greenpeace, which statement is not true?
   (A) Industrialized countries are dumping toxic waste in Taiwan.
   (B) The toxic waste comes from Britain and the U.S..
   (C) Much of the toxic waste comes from Britain and the U.S..
   (D) 4000 tons of waste materials were imported in 1992.

2. The United States
   (A) recycles the goods and sends them to Asian countries.
   (B) has the goods recycled in Asia and then dumps them.
   (C) recycles "recyclable" goods in the U.S. and sends the rest to Asian countries.
   (D) does not recycle in the U.S. but sends "recyclable" wastes to Asian countries.

3. The R.O.C's environmental protection laws
   (A) prohibit the importation of waste materials.
   (B) allow the importation of materials which become toxic through burning.
   (C) allow the importation of some toxic materials as long as they are burned after.
   (D) prohibit the importation of burnt toxic materials.

台灣成為有毒物質傾倒之地

〔中國郵報〕國際環境保護單位──綠色和平組織警告說道，台灣正快速成為工業化國家傾倒毒物的地方。

自立晚報昨天報導，綠色和平組織於三月十一日寫信給中華民國環保署，信中提到光是在一九九二年前六個月中，台灣就從美國和英國進口了超過兩千噸的有毒物質。

根據綠色和平組織研究指出，在美國所謂的「再生」物品，並不是真正的在當地再生利用，相反的，可供再生的廢料運到了台灣、南韓、巴基斯坦、中國大陸和菲律賓。

中華民國環境保育法只有禁止進口有毒物質，但卻允許進口塑膠，以及其他在燃燒後會釋放毒氣的物質。

本地新聞界宣稱：國外廢物大量流入台灣，已降低了國內垃圾的價格，並使國內製造業者和消費者因回收利潤低，而降低回收意願。

** dump 〔dʌmp〕 v. 傾倒　　　toxic 〔'tɑksɪk〕 adj. 有毒的
industrialized 〔ɪn'dʌstrɪəl,aɪzd〕 adj. 工業化的
import 〔ɪm'port〕 v. 進口　recycle 〔ri'saɪkl〕 v. 再生利用
bar 〔bɑr〕 v. 禁止　substance 〔'sʌbstəns〕 n. 物質
plastic 〔'plæstɪk〕 n. 塑膠　　influx 〔'ɪn,flʌks〕 n. 流入
domestic 〔də'mɛstɪk〕 adj. 國內的
consumer 〔kən'sumə, -'sjumə〕n. 消費者
margin 〔'mɑrdʒɪn〕 n. 餘額　　　assert 〔ə'sɝt〕 v. 宣稱

Sea warning on edging Yancy issued

Compiled by
The China Post

The Central Weather Bureau issued a sea warning last night on typhoon Yancy which is edging its way toward Taiwan.

The bureau warned ships working in eastern Taiwan waters and the Bashi Channel to be careful of the strong winds brought by Yancy.

Yancy may also bring boons to drought-plagued regions as it was expected to unleash rain in its path, added the forecasters.

Yancy's center was located at 20.6 north latitude and 128.4 east longitude at 4:30 p.m. yesterday or 810 kilometers east of Hengchun, southern Taiwan.

Yancy was moving westward at 15 kph and its sustained wind was estimated at 28 meters per second.

If Yancy brings rains as predicted, a program to create artificial rain in the Keelung area will be delayed or canceled, officials said.

The water company imposed restriction on Keelung residents as a stubborn drought has been draining its major reservoir for over two months.

解答 ☞ p. 266

1. One effect of the Yancy typhoon
   (A) would be positive, helping relieve the drought by raining.
   (B) would be negative, unleashing rain in drought regions.
   (C) would be negative, with high winds preventing rain.
   (D) would be positive, unleashing boons in its path.

2. If Yancy brings rain as predicted,
   (A) the water company will impose restrictions.
   (B) high winds will keep the typhoon moving westwards.
   (C) artificial rain will be created to cancel the drought.
   (D) the artificial rain program will be put back or canceled.

3. As a result of the drought, the water company has been
   (A) closely monitoring the path of typhoons.
   (B) imposing water restrictions on residents.
   (C) draining its major reservoirs for over two months.
   (D) imposing restrictions on stubborn Keelung residents.

氣象局發布楊西颱風海上警報

〔中國郵報〕中央氣象局昨夜發布楊西颱風海上警報，楊西颱風正慢慢接近台灣。

氣象局警告在台灣東部海域及巴士海峽作業的船隻謹防楊西所帶來的強風。

預報員還指出，楊西可能會為乾旱災區降甘霖。因為一般預料它會沿途降下大量雨水。

昨天下午四點三十分，楊西颱風的中心位置在北緯二十點六度，東經一百二十八點四度，也就是距台灣南部恆春東方八百一十公里處。

楊西以每小時十五公里的速度向西行進，估計其平均風速為每秒二十八公尺。

官員表示，如果楊西如預期帶來大量雨水，基隆地區的人造雨計畫將會延後或取消。

水公司對基隆居民採取限水措施，因為兩個多月來，頑強的乾旱已使它主要的水庫日趨乾涸。

**　edge〔ɛdʒ〕v.（使）慢慢移動　　　issue〔'ɪʃjʊ〕v. 發布
The Central Weather Bureau 中央氣象局　waters〔'wɑtəz〕n.pl. 海域
the Bashi Channel 巴士海峽　　boon〔bun〕n. 贈物；恩典
drought-plagued〔'draʊt'plegd〕adj. 遭受乾旱的
region〔'ridʒən〕n. 地區　　unleash〔ʌn'liʃ〕v. 降下；發洩
latitude〔'lætə,tjud〕n. 緯度　　longitude〔'landʒə,tjud〕n. 經度
sustain〔sə'sten〕v. 持續　　estimate〔'ɛstə,met〕v. 估計
predict〔prɪ'dɪkt〕v. 預測　　impose〔ɪm'poz〕v. 加於

英文報紙必備氣象用語

◇ Central Weather Bureau 中央氣象局

◇ weather report 氣象報告　　　fair〔fɛr〕*adj.* 晴朗的

◇ cloudy〔'klaʊdɪ〕*adj.* 多雲的

◇ overcast〔,ovɚ'kæst〕*adj.* 陰的

◇ showery〔'ʃaʊərɪ〕*adj.* 陣雨的　　　rainy〔'renɪ〕*adj.* 多雨的

◇ temperature〔'tɛmprətʃɚ〕*n.* 溫度

◇ Celsius〔'sɛlsɪəs〕*adj.* 攝氏的

◇ Fahrenheit〔'færən,haɪt〕*adj.* 華氏的

◇ front〔frʌnt〕*n.* 鋒面

◇ low（high）pressure 低（高）氣壓　　　air mass 氣團

◇ typhoon〔taɪ'fun〕*n.* 颱風（發生於中日菲一帶）

◇ hurricane〔'hɝɪ,ken〕*n.* 颶風（發生於墨西哥灣和西印度群島間）

◇ tornado〔tɔr'nedo〕*n.* 龍捲風　　　rainfall〔'ren,fɔl〕*n.* 降雨量

◇ downpour〔'daʊn,pɔr〕*n.* ; rain cats and dogs 傾盆大雨

◇ thunder storm 雷雨　　　drizzle〔'drɪzl̩〕*n.* 毛毛雨

◇ monsoon〔mɑn'sun〕*n.* 雨季

◇ muggy weather 悶熱天氣　　　freakish weather 反常天氣

◇ moisture〔'mɔɪstʃɚ〕*n.* 濕氣

◇ humidity〔hju'mɪdətɪ〕*n.* 濕度

◇ density〔'dɛnsətɪ〕*n.* 密度

◇ drought〔draʊt〕*n.* 旱災　　　flood〔flʌd〕*n.* 水災

Health   *Sunday Apr. 25*

Babies at risk from smoking moms

Reuter

London —Mothers who smoke and share their beds with their babies are putting them at risk of cot death, according to New Zealand research published recently.

The numbers of cot deaths has been reduced by having babies sleep on their backs rather than their stomachs. Previous research has also indicated a possible link between bedsharing and sudden infant death.

The researchers from the universities of Auckland and Otago studied 393 sudden infant deaths from 1987 to 1990.

They concluded that a further fifth of such deaths might be prevented if mothers did not expose their children to cigarette smoke or bring their babies into bed with them.

解答 ☞ p. 266

1. Why are babies at risk from cot death?
   (A) Sleeping in cots when their mother smokes.
   (B) Sharing a bed with a mother and smoking.
   (C) Sharing a bed with a mother who is smoking.
   (D) Sharing a cot with a mother who smokes.

2. In order to reduce the numbers of cot deaths,
   (A) babies have been made to sleep on their stomachs in cots.
   (B) babies have been removed from smoky atmospheres.
   (C) babies have been made to sleep on their backs instead of stomachs.
   (D) babies have been separated from mothers who smoke.

3. There is a possible link between
   (A) bed sharing and smoking
   (B) a baby sleeping on its back and a mother smoking.
   (C) a baby sleeping on its stomach and a mother smoking.
   (D) a baby sleeping with a mother smoking and cot death.

4. A further fifth of cot deaths would
   (A) possibly not happen without bed-sharing and a smoky atmosphere.
   (B) possibly not happen if mothers didn't smoke.
   (C) definitely be prevented by sleeping alone in a cot.
   (D) definitely happen because of bed-sharing.

Focus

●*成長相關字彙*

infant 〔ˈɪnfənt〕 *n.* 嬰兒；幼兒(未滿七歲)

puberty 〔ˈpjubətɪ〕 *n.* 青春期

crack 〔kræk〕 *n.* 變聲

precocity 〔prɪˈkɑsətɪ〕 *n.* 早熟

minor 〔ˈmaɪnɚ〕 *adj.* 未成年的

|||||||||||||||||||||||||||||||||||||||||||||||||||||||||||||||||

母親抽煙危害嬰兒

〔路透社〕倫敦電——根據紐西蘭最近發表的研究報告顯示，母親抽煙，又與嬰兒同床，將會使嬰兒有在床上猝死的危險。

讓嬰兒以仰睡取代臥睡,已經減少了嬰兒死於床上的事件。先前的研究也指出，嬰兒猝死可能和與人同床有關。

奧克蘭大學及奧塔哥大學的研究人員，對一九八七至一九九〇年，三百九十三件嬰兒猝死加以研究。

他們推論，假如母親不讓小孩暴露於二手煙中，或不把嬰兒帶到自己的床上同睡，那麼，有五分之一以上的此類死亡，將可避免。

** risk〔rɪsk〕n. 危險 　　cot〔kɑt〕n. 嬰兒床
indicate〔'ɪndə,ket〕v. 指出 　infant〔'ɪnfənt〕n. 嬰兒
expose〔ɪk'spoz〕v. 暴露 　　removal〔rɪ'muvl̩〕n. 排除
maternal〔mə'tɜnl̩〕adj. 母親的
theoretically〔,θiə'rɛtɪkl̩ɪ〕adv. 理論上

Life　　　　　　　　　　　*Monday Dec 27*

N. Europe mops up

Reuter

Amsterdam, Dec. 26 — Thousands of Dutch, German and Belgian citizens who had to flee from water soaked homes at Christmas began cleaning up on Sunday after the worst flooding in northwestern Europe in decades.

Rivers swollen by torrential rain were reported retreating in the heaviest hit areas of the southeastern Netherlands and low-lying riverside parts of Germany and Belgium.

At least seven people were killed in the region as a result of the weather in the run-up to Christmas.

Then, freezing conditions on Saturday night and Sunday morning made roads treacherous. Dutch and Belgian police reported 42 accidents in the overnight period.

解答 ☞ p.266

1. When the water flooded their homes, the citizens
   (A) were forced to clean their homes at Christmas.
   (B) were forced to retreat from swollen rivers.
   (C) were forced to retreat from low-lying areas.
   (D) were forced to flee their homes.

2. Rivers were reported to be
   (A) swelling with torrential rain.
   (B) soaking the homes of many people.
   (C) going down in the worst affected areas.
   (D) particularly hitting areas of the southeastern Nether-
       lands and low-lying areas of Belgium and Germany.

3. At least seven people were killed
   (A) running up to the Christmas flood.
   (B) in the riverside regions.
   (C) retreating from the flood.
   (D) in the period leading to Christmas.

4. According to the article, what caused 42 accidents?
   (A) Roads made slippery through freezing conditions.
   (B) The treachery of the road.
   (C) The Police were busy with the flood and unable to
       prevent them.
   (D) People fleeing the floods overnight.

收拾北歐殘局

〔路透社〕阿姆斯特丹，十二月二十六日電——在聖誕節，有數以千計的荷蘭人、德國人和比利時人得從浸水的房子裏逃出。他們在星期天，也就是北歐數十年來最嚴重的一場洪水氾濫之後，開始做清理工作。

據報導，豪雨造成的河水暴漲，目前正從災情最嚴重的地區消退中，也就是荷蘭東南方，以及德國和比利時河床水位較低的地方。

當時正逢聖誕節籌備期間，該區至少有七人因氣候喪生。

之後週六晚上以及週日清晨嚴寒的天氣，使得一些路段十分危險。據荷蘭與比利時的警方報導，在一夜之間，便有四十二起意外事件發生。

** ***mop up*** 清理；收拾

Amsterdam〔ˋæmstɚˏdæm〕*n.* 阿姆斯特丹（荷蘭首都）

Dutch〔dʌtʃ〕*n.* 荷蘭人　　Belgian〔ˋbɛldʒən〕*n.* 比利時人

flee〔fli〕*v.* 逃走　　　soak〔sok〕*v.* 浸；泡

decade〔ˋdɛked〕*n.* 十年　　swell〔swɛl〕*v.* 高漲

torrential〔tɔˋrɛnʃəl〕*adj.* 猛烈的　　retreat〔rɪˋtrit〕*v.* 撤退

Netherlands〔ˋnɛðɚləndz〕*n.* 荷蘭　　***as a result of*** 由於～的結果

run-up〔ˋrʌnˏʌp〕*n.* 籌備期間

treacherous〔ˋtrɛtʃərəs〕*adj.* 危險的

overnight〔ˋovɚˋnaɪt〕*adv.* 一夜之間

Stress increases risk of early death

By Dan Hurley
Medical Tribune New Service

Getting divorced, fired or charged with a crime could greatly increase a middle-aged man's risk of dying young, Swedish researchers have found.

The good news, however, is that middle-aged men who have recently been through stressful life events may be able to protect themselves from an increased risk of death by maintaining close contacts with friends and family members.

For those without close support, the relationship between the stressful events and the risk of death was striking in the Swedish study:

— Having a family member with a serious illness, or even just having a serious concern about a family member, doubled the 50-year-old men's risk of dying in the next seven years.

— Getting divorced or separated before turning 50 tripled their risk of death.

— Being forced to move from their house tripled their risk of an early death, as did being in serious financial trouble.

解答☞ p.266

1. A middle-aged man's risk of dying young
    (A) is caused by divorce, losing a job, or being charged with a crime.
    (B) would be lessened by avoiding problems in life.
    (C) is greatly increased near fifty years of age.
    (D) is greatly increased by stressful life events.

2. Middle-aged men may be able to protect themselves
    (A) through supporting themselves against family problems.
    (B) through close contact with friends and family members.
    (C) through a good social security system.
    (D) through having a good social life.

3. According to the article, what was striking?
    (A) How much social support there could be for middle-aged men.
    (B) How the risk of death was supported by life-events.
    (C) How the increased risk of death was tied to lack of close support.
    (D) How a middle-aged man could survive three life events in one year.

4. The risks to middle-aged man's health from stressful events
    (A) depend very much on his level of support from his family and friends.
    (B) are beyond his control, becausae they come from life events.
    (C) can be controlled through being aware of the effects of life events on health.
    (D) double or triple depending on how serious the concern of the middle-aged man is.

壓力增加早死之虞

〔醫藥論壇新聞中心〕瑞典研究員發現，離婚、被開除或被控訴將大幅增加中年男子早死的危險。

然而，好消息是，近來生活中一直遭遇壓力的中年男子，可藉著和朋友家人親密的聯繫來保護自己，而不用擔心死亡危險性的增加。

瑞典的一項研究顯示：對於那些沒有家人朋友鼓勵的中年男性而言，壓力事件和死亡的危險性關係密切。

——家人患有嚴重疾病，或只是極度擔憂家人，將會使五十歲的中年男子，在往後七年中，其死亡危險性較常人高出一倍。

——即將邁入五十歲而離婚或分居的中年男子，其死亡危險性是一般人的三倍。

——被迫搬家或有嚴重經濟困難的中年男子，其死亡危險性亦是一般人的三倍。

** tribune 〔'trɪbjun〕 n. 論壇　　risk 〔rɪsk〕 n. 危險
divorce 〔də'vors〕 v. 離婚　　charge 〔tʃɑrdʒ〕 v. 指控
Swedish 〔'swidɪʃ〕 adj. 瑞典的
contact 〔'kɑntækt〕 n. 接觸
striking 〔'straɪkɪŋ〕 adj. 顯著的　　separate 〔'sɛpə,ret〕 v. 分開
triple 〔'trɪpḷ〕 v. (使)成三倍
financial 〔faɪ'nænʃəl〕 adj. 財務的

Longevity   *Thursday Sept. 22*

World's oldest woman turns 119

The world's oldest woman, Jeanne Calment, turned 119 and vowed to be around for birthday celebrations next year.

"I have promised to live to be 120. I'll make an effort," the frail Frenchwoman said as she blew out 19 candles on her birthday cake at a retirement home in southern France.

Calment, who boasts an entry in the Guinness Book of World Records, is not keen on the publicity. "I'm not a phenomenon. I'm an ordinary woman," she said. She has outlived 17 French presidents. She married in the 19th century and her daughter, Yvonne, died 60 years ago at age 36.

解答 ☞ p.266

■ The world's oldest woman
(A) married in 1900s.
(B) lived with her daughter.
(C) was unhappy about her longevity.
(D) promised to live to be 120.

金氏紀錄中的人瑞

　　世界上最高齡的婦女葛門年近一百一十九歲，她並立誓要過下一次的生日。

　　這位病弱的法國婦人在法國南部的養老院過生日，當她吹熄十九根蠟燭時表示：「我已說了要活到一百廿歲。我一定要努力做到。」

　　已被列入金氏世界紀錄的葛門並不喜歡出風頭，她說：「我並不是什麼特別的人物，我只是普通的女人。」她一生經歷了十七任法國總統。她在十九世紀結婚，而她的女兒依凡於六十年前去世，死時只有三十六歲。

** vow〔vaʊ〕v. 立誓　　*make an effort* 努力
blow out 吹熄　　retirement〔rɪˈtaɪrmənt〕n. 退休
boast〔bost〕v. 擁有～而自豪　　entry〔ˈɛntrɪ〕n. 列入
the Guinness Book of World Records 金氏世界紀錄（每年蒐集各
　種破世界紀錄的人、事、物）
be keen on 熱衷於　　publicity〔ˌpʌbˈlɪsətɪ〕n. 出風頭
phonomenon〔fəˈnɑməˌnɑn〕n. 非凡的人
outlive〔aʊtˈlɪv〕v. 比～長壽

phenomenon

Part 6

Economy & Trade 經濟貿易

Economy

Regional growth seen helping fuel economy

Singapore expects sustained economic growth of between six and eight percent next year with help from robust regional economies and diversified export markets, a senior government spokesman said recently.

"Our growth will benefit from the regional economic growth (and is) expected at 6-8 percent next year," he told a news conference.

Singapore's third-quarter economic survey showed its economy grew nine percent on average through September, compared to 5.8 percent last year. A major source of growth was exports.

Regional growth in mainland China, South Korea, Hong Kong and Taiwan would help Singapore even if the industrialized countries' growth rate lags, the Ministry of Trade and Industry spokesman said.

Singapore's strength is that it does not depend on a single market for its exports, he said.

解答☞ p.266

1. Sustained economic growth suggests
   (A) a rapidly rising growth rate.
   (B) a continuing, steady growth rate.
   (C) a wildly fluctuating growth rate.
   (D) a continuously declining growth rate.

2. What has been a strong sector contributing to Singapore's growth?
   (A) the financial sector
   (B) the telecommunications sector
   (C) the export sector
   (D) the government sector

3. Singapore's regional trade is best described as trade with
   (A) newly industrializing countries with rapid growth rates.
   (B) mature economies with large import demands.
   (C) third world countries.
   (D) technologically advanced nations.

4. What is Singapore's economic health supported by?
   (A) its proximity to friendly trading nations
   (B) its high level of domestic growth
   (C) its close relationship with large, mature economies
   (D) its growing exports to a wide variety of countries

區域成長有助於經濟發展

　　新加坡一名資深政府發言人最近指出，因為強勁的區域經濟、及分散的外銷市場，預料該國明年的經濟，成長率可望維持在百分之六至百分之八之間。

　　他在記者會中指出：「由於區域經濟的成長，明年本國的經濟將可成長百分之六至百分之八。」

　　新加坡第三季經濟調查顯示，其經濟至九月份為止，平均成長了百分之九，相較於去年的百分之五點八。成長的主因之一是外銷。

　　新加坡工商部發言人表示，即使工業國家的成長率緩慢，中國大陸、南韓、香港和台灣的區域性成長，也將有助於新加坡的經濟成長。

　　他說：新加坡的實力所在，便是它不只依賴單一的外銷市場。

** regional〔ˈridʒənḷ〕*adj.* 區域性的　　fuel〔ˈfjuəl〕*v.* 促成
　　sustained〔səˈstend〕*adj.* 持續不變的
　　robust〔roˈbʌst〕*adj.* 強大的
　　diversified〔daɪˈvɝsə,faɪd〕*adj.* 分散的；多種的
　　export〔ˈɛksport〕*adj.* 外銷的
　　news conference 記者會
　　survey〔ˈsɝve〕*n.* 調查　　lag〔læg〕*v.* 落後

Forex

Monday Feb. 28

New highs for foreign exchange

The export and import foreign exchange settlements last month reached US$ 8.394 billion and US$ 7.563 billion, respectively, both hitting new monthly highs, the Central Bank of China said yesterday.

Statistics also indicated that aggregate foreign exchange incomes from Taiwan's exports totaled US$ 87.99 billion in 1993, up 3.9 percent from a year earlier. Forex expenses on imports came to US$ 74.1 billion in the past year, up three percent from a year ago. The resultant forex surplus totaled US$ 13.89 billion.

解答☞ p.266

The import foreign exchange settlements last month reached

(A) US$ 8.394 billion. (B) US$ 7.563 billion.
(C) US$ 87.99 billion. (D) US$ 74.1 billion.

外滙再創新高點

央行昨天表示，依據上個月的結算結果，進出口外滙分別達到八十三億九千四百萬美元與七十五億六千三百萬美元，再創每月外滙進出的新高點。

統計資料也顯示，一九九三年中華民國因出口而賺取的外滙收入總額爲八百七十九億九千萬美元，比前一年高出3.9％。而去年因進口而支出的外滙高達七百四十億一千萬美元，比前年高了三個百分點。外滙存底的總數爲一百三十八億九千萬美元。

** *foreign exchange* 外滙　　settlement〔ˈsɛtlmənt〕*n.* 結算
respectively〔rɪˈspɛktɪvlɪ〕*adv.* 分別地
statistics〔stəˈtɪstɪks〕*n. pl.* 統計資料
aggregate〔ˈægrɪgɪt〕*n.* 總數　　income〔ˈɪn,kʌm〕*n.* 收入
total〔ˈtotl〕*v.* 總計
forex（＝*for*eign *ex*change）外滙
expense〔ɪkˈspɛns〕*n.* 花費
resultant〔rɪˈzʌltənt〕*adj.* 結果的
surplus〔ˈsɝpləs〕*n.* 剩餘

Stock market

Thursday Jan. 6

Market bullish as year begins

By Pao Chieh-sheng
The China Post

The Taiwan Stock Exchange got off to a heady start for the new year yesterday as the weighted index boomed 346.28 points to close up 5.7 percent at 6,416.84, the highest level in the past 31 months.

Trading commenced yesterday after a five-day break for the new year holiday. Some 3.336 billion shares of stock changed hands, resulting in the highest turnover in 45 months. Yesterday's trading was valued at NT$145.02 billion.

Financial shares led the way in gains during the day's trading, rising in value by nearly seven percent. Other sectors posting strong growth included transportation, electronics and textiles.

解答 ☞ p. 266

1. What happened to the market at the beginning of the year ?
   (A) It reached a 31 month low.
   (B) It reached a 31 month peak.
   (C) It was highly volatile.
   (D) It saw new highs for large companies.

2. A bullish market
   (A) suggests optimism.
   (B) suggests pessimism.
   (C) favors institutional investors.
   (D) favors corporate takeovers.

3. What is turnover ?
   (A) the strength of market forces
   (B) the volatility of the market
   (C) the volume of shares traded
   (D) the volume of shares issued

4. What was the leading sector in percentage gain ?
   (A) electronics   (B) financial
   (C) the stock market   (D) the NT dollar

新的一年股市行情看漲

〔中國郵報〕昨天台灣的股市交易，新的一年就出現了令人興奮的開始。指數暴漲三百四十六點二八點，收盤時為百分之五點七，指數達六千四百一十六點八四點，是過去三十一個月以來的最高點，漲幅為百分之五點七。

新年假期休市五天之後，股市昨天又恢復交易。大約有三十三億三千六百萬股的股票交割，總成交量為四十五個月以來最高點。昨天的總成交額為新台幣一千四百五十億二千萬元。

昨天金融股呈現長紅，上漲了將近七個百分點。其他明顯上揚的類股還包括運輸、電子、以及紡織股。

** bullish〔'bʊlɪʃ〕*adj.*看漲的　　heady〔'hɛdɪ〕*adj.*令人興奮的
weighted〔'wetɪd〕*adj.*有利的　　boom〔bum〕*v.*暴漲
index〔'ɪndɛks〕*n.*指數　　trading〔'tredɪŋ〕*n.*交易
commence〔kə'mɛns〕*v.*開始　　break〔brek〕*n.*休息
share〔ʃɛr〕*n.*股份；股票　　stock〔stɑk〕*n.*股票
turnover〔'tɝn,ovɚ〕*n.*成交額　　value〔'vælju〕*v.*評價
financial shares 金融股　　*lead the way* 領頭前進
gains〔'genz〕*n. pl.*利益　　sector〔'sɛktɚ〕*n.*部門
post〔post〕*v.*公告　　transportation〔,trænspɚ'teʃən〕*n.*運輸
electronics〔ɪ,lɛk'trɑnɪks〕*n.*電子學
textile〔'tɛkstaɪl〕*n.*紡織品

英文報紙必備財經用語

◊ finance〔fəˈnæns, ˈfaɪnæns〕*n.* 財政

◊ economy〔ɪˈkɑnəmɪ〕*n.* 經濟　economic crisis 經濟恐慌

◊ economic expansion 經濟起飛

◊ economic stability 經濟穩定

◊ currency〔ˈkɝənsɪ〕*n.*（現在通用的）貨幣

◊ deficit financing 財政赤字

◊ inflation〔ɪnˈfleʃən〕*n.* 通貨膨脹

◊ depression〔dɪˈprɛʃən〕*n.* ; economic slump 不景氣

◊ excess of imports 入超　　excess of exports 出超

◊ surplus〔ˈsɝplʌs〕*n.* ; favorable trade balance 順差

◊ deficit〔ˈdɛfəsɪt〕*n.* ; unfavorable trade balance 逆差

◊ consortium〔kənˈsɔrʃɪəm, -tɪəm〕*n.* 國際財團

◊ standand of living 生活水準

◊ living index 生活指數　　　　price index 物價指數

◊ gross national product（G.N.P.）國民生產毛額

◊ per capita income 國民所得　　stock market 股票市場

◊ stock exchange house 證券交易所

◊ unemployment〔ˌʌnɪmˈplɔɪmənt〕*n.* 失業（狀態）

◊ opening price 開盤　　closing price 收盤

◊ rising〔ˈraɪzɪŋ〕*n.* 上漲　　soaring〔ˈsorɪŋ〕*n.* 飛漲

◊ raising the limit 漲停板　　falling〔ˈfɔlɪŋ〕*n.* 下跌

◇ break〔brek〕*n*. 暴跌　　slump〔slʌmp〕*n*. 狂跌

◇ investor〔ɪn'vɛstɚ〕*n*. 投資者

◇ agiotage〔'ædʒətɪdʒ, 'ædʒɪə-〕*n*. 買賣股票

◇ stock dividend 配股

◇ manipulate〔mə'nɪpjə,let〕*v*. 操縱

◇ stock income tax 證券交易稅　　bear〔bɛr〕*n*. 做空頭者

◇ speculator〔'spɛkjə,letɚ〕*n*. 投機者

◇ dealing in futures 期貨

◇ automatic cash dispenser 自動提款機

◇ World Bank I.B.R.D.（International Bank for
Reconstruction & Development）世界開發銀行

◇ IMF（International Monetary Fund）國際貨幕基金

◇ exchequer〔ɪks't∫ɛkɚ, 'ɛkst∫ɛkɚ〕*n*. 國庫；財源

◇ Central Bank 中央銀行　　cooperative bank 合作金庫

◇ commercial bank 商業銀行

◇ credit cooperation 信用合作社　　fiscal year 會計年度

◇ Wall Street 紐約華爾街　　deposit〔dɪ'pɑzɪt〕*n*. 存款

◇ taxation〔tæks'e∫ən〕*n*. 課稅

◇ commodity〔kə'mɑdətɪ〕*n*. 商品

◇ transaction〔træns'æk∫ən〕*n*. 交易

◇ allowance〔ə'lauəns〕*n*. 津貼

◇ foreign currency 外幣

International trade　　*Friday Dec. 29*

Import growth rate put at 11.4%

Taiwan's annual import growth rate averaged 11.4 percent between 1980 and 1991, for the highest increase of its kind in the world.

The same tallies indicated that the island's average yearly export growth rate stood at 10.3 percent for the past 12 years, the ninth highest in the world.

Meanwhile, Taiwan's average yearly expansion rate in gross national product during the 12-year period ranked the second in the world, at 6.4 percent, next only to South Korea's 8.7 percent.

In terms of average annual inflation rate, Taiwan took the 12th lowest place at 3.1 percent. The lowest rate, at a negative level of 3.1 percent, was recorded by Oman.

解答☞ p.266

1. What happened to Taiwan's annual import growth?
   (A) It grew faster than in any other country.
   (B) It produced the largest volume of imports in the world after 12 years.
   (C) It was superseded only by that of South Korea.
   (D) It caused more goods to be imported than exported over 12 years.

2. What happens with a negative inflation rate of 3.1 percent?
   (A) Prices increase greatly.
   (B) Prices increase moderately.
   (C) The results for the economy would be very negative.
   (D) Prices would decrease moderately.

進口成長率據估計為 11.4%

　　台灣在一九八〇年至一九九一年之間，平均每年進口成長率為 11.4%，居全世界第一位。

　　同樣的計算方式也指出，在過去十二年以來，台灣年平均出口成長率為 10.3%，全世界排名第九。

　　同時台灣在十二年內，每年平均國民生產毛額增加率為 6.4%，居世界第二位，僅次於南韓的 8.7%。

　　就年度平均通貨膨脹率而言，台灣為 3.1%，在通貨膨脹率最低的國家中，排名第十二。而通貨膨脹率最低的國家為安曼，其通貨膨脹率為 − 3.1%。

**　annual〔'ænjʊəl〕*adj.* 每年的　　tally〔'tælɪ〕*n.* 計算
　　expansion〔ɪk'spænʃən〕*n.* 擴張
　　gross national product（*GNP*）國民生產毛額
　　rank〔ræŋk〕*v.* 位居　　*in terms of* 就⋯的觀點
　　inflation〔ɪn'fleʃən〕*n.* 通貨膨脹
　　negative〔'nɛgətɪv〕*adj.* 負的　　Oman〔o'mæn〕*n.* 安曼

Salary

Salary hikes for production workers at a nine-year low

Salaries of workers in the manufacturing sector only increased 6.96 percent last year, the lowest in nine years, announced the Ministry of Economic Affairs.

The value of the country's total production only increased 3.44 percent, the lowest increase in the past decade, officials added.

Ministry officials said these figures were affected by the number of companies moving abroad to do basic production. As companies moved away, they took production with them which were not replaced.

Job hunters' lack of interest in production jobs contributed to the slow increase in the nation's production, the officials said. They said most job-seekers preferred to work in the less-laborious service industry.

The slow global growth rate also affected the economy here, resulting in lower production and only small increases in salaries of workers.

Ministry officials suggested automation and increased quality as the only ways production can increase in Taiwan.

解答 ☞ p.266

1. The figures for the past year were affected by
   (A) production moving away from Taiwan and not being replaced.
   (B) competition from overseas.
   (C) the lack of basic production in Taiwan.
   (D) higher productivity abroad.

2. Job hunters preferred to
   (A) seek work in higher-paying jobs.
   (B) work in less physically demanding occupations.
   (C) seek more interesting work than production.
   (D) wait for improved job market conditions.

3. In order to restore production growth,
   (A) Taiwan shouldn't relocate factories abroad.
   (B) Taiwan should improve its production image.
   (C) Taiwan should automate more and improve product quality.
   (D) Taiwan should increase the salary of production workers.

製造業工人薪資調幅為九年來最低

經濟部宣布，去年製造業部門工人薪資只增加了百分之六點九六，是九年來最低的一次。

經濟部官員表示，國家生產總額只增加了百分之三點四四，是過去十年來成長度最低的。

經濟部官員指出，這些數據，受到基礎製造工廠外移的數量影響。當工廠外移，產量也移走，而無以取代。

官員們表示，求職者對生產業工作興趣缺缺，因而使國內產量慢慢下降。他們指出，大部分的求職者較喜歡從事勞力較少的服務業。

全球緩慢的成長率也影響了本地的經濟，造成產量較低，而工人薪水只有小幅增加。

經濟部官員建議，自動化及品質的提昇，是增加台灣製造產量的唯一途徑。

** hike〔haɪk〕v. 抬高
manufacturing〔ˌmænjəˈfæktʃərɪŋ〕n. 製造業
sector〔ˈsɛktɚ〕n. 部門
announce〔əˈnaʊns〕v. 宣布
the Ministry of Economic Affairs 經濟部
contribute to 造成　　***result in*** 導致
automation〔ˌɔtəˈmeʃən〕n. 自動化

Stock market   *thursday Mar. 3*

Market dramatics continue

Compiled by The China Post

More dramatics occurred on the stock market yesterday as trading recorded a three year-high of NT$185.8 billion in turnover, while stocks fluctuated to a heart-stopping 436 points before closing up 38 points at 6,454.52.

Heavy profit-taking following Tuesday's 346 points was responsible for the wild swings which saw the market climb 112 points before buying pressure set in at 6,720. Total market volume reached an all-time record of 4.23 billion.

At the close, 65 concerns hits the 7-percent upper ceiling, while 29 fell to the ground limit. Advancers outran losers by 132 to 194, with 17 issues remaining unchanged.

"There has been a lot of buying pressure on the Taiex for a long time and it was a matter of seeing when the whole thing would crack," one analyst said.

解答☞ p.266

1. What was the situation at the close of trading?
   (A) The net result was positive with advancers
       outweighing decliners.
   (B) The net result was mixed with advancers about
       equal with decliners.
   (C) A large number of stocks were at their maximum
       level.
   (D) There was a great variation with many stocks at
       their maximum and many at their base figure.

2. Why was the Taiex ready to crack?
   (A) There were too many decliners.
   (B) There was too much fluctuation in the market.
   (C) A large number of stocks were at their maximum
       level.
   (D) Buying pressure had built up for a long time.

3. Why did the market swing wildly?
   (A) because of profit-taking
   (B) because of an all-time record volume
   (C) because of its climbing 112 points
   (D) because of buying pressure

股市仍持續震盪的走勢

〔中國郵報〕昨天股市仍呈現震盪的走勢。據報導，昨天股市成交量爲新台幣一千八百五十八億元，是三年來最高點。股票指數在收盤前，曾一度上揚四百三十六點，終場收盤時，指數爲六千四百五十四點五二點，上揚了三十八點。

由於星期二股票上揚了三百四十六點，投資者獲利之後，買壓尚未介入之前，指數就上升了一百一十二點，達到六千七百二十點，成交總值創下空前的記錄——新台幣四十二億三千萬元。

收盤時，有六十五家商行的漲幅，達到百分之七的上限，有二十九家則爲跌停板。上升的有一百三十二家，下跌的一百九十四家，有十七家持平。

有位分析家指出：「台灣的股市長久以來都有許多的買壓，問題就在於觀察股市何時會崩盤。」

**　dramatics〔drə'mætɪks〕*n.* 戲劇性的行爲
　　turnover〔'tɜn,ovɚ〕*n.* 成交額
　　fluctuate〔'flʌktʃʊ,et〕*v.* 變動
　　swing〔swɪŋ〕*v.* 擺動；轉變　　volume〔'vɑljəm〕*n.* 交易量
　　all-time〔'ɔl,taɪm〕*adj.* 空前的
　　concern〔kən'sɜn〕*n.* 商行
　　advancer〔əd'vænsɚ〕*n.* 上升者　　issue〔'ɪʃʊ〕*n.* 發行
　　Taiex（＝*Tai*wan *Ex*change）　台灣股市交易；台灣證券交易所
　　crack〔kræk〕*v.* 崩潰　　analyst〔'ænl̩ɪst〕*n.* 分析家

International Trade

Friday Apr. 15

Over 30 nations have barriers against Taiwan

Compiled by The China Post

Over 30 countries are imposing tariff or non-tariff trade barriers against Taiwan products, according to a major local industrial association.

The Chinese National Federation of Industries（CNFI）indicated in a recent survey that over a dozen Taiwan-made industrial products, including steel plates, foods, computers, car components and telecommunication products are faced with various unnatural obstructions when sold in foreign markets.

Japan, the United States, Australia, several countries in Europe, Thailand, Malaysia, Indonesia and the Philippines have more artificial curbs on imports than other countries have against Taiwan goods, the report said.

解答 ☞ p.266

1. According to a local industrial association,
   (A) thirty countries are preventing Taiwanese goods from entering their markets.
   (B) various tax and non-tax obstacles to Taiwanese products are making market access difficult in a large number of countries.
   (C) thirty countries are unfairly discriminating against Taiwan trade.
   (D) thirty countries have preferential trade with Taiwan.

2. To curb means :
   (A) to enforce
   (B) to restrict
   (C) to prohibit
   (D) to establish

3. How might an unnatural obstruction best be described?
   (A) Something which enables easy access.
   (B) Something which artificially favors access.
   (C) Something which artificially denies access.
   (D) Something which is trade neutral.

超過三十個國家對台灣實行貿易障礙

〔中國郵報〕根據某主要地方工會指出，超過三十個國家以課徵關稅、或採非關稅貿易等阻礙來抵制台灣產品。

中華國家工業聯盟（CNFI）在一項最近的調查指出，超過十二種台灣製的產品，包括鋼製餐具、食品、電腦、汽車零件、以及一些電信產品在售往海外市場時，面臨到許多不合情理的阻礙。

報導並指出，日本、美國、澳洲，幾個歐洲國家，泰國、馬來西亞、印尼、以及菲律賓，比其他各國更刻意抵制台灣產品。

** barrier〔ˈbærɪɚ〕n. 阻礙　　compile〔kəmˈpaɪl〕v. 編輯
impose〔ɪmˈpoz〕v. 課（稅）
tariff〔ˈtærɪf〕n. 關稅（率）　　local〔ˈlokl̩〕adj. 地方的
association〔ə͵sosɪˈeʃən〕n. 工會；協會
federation〔͵fɛdəˈreʃən〕n. 聯合；聯盟
component〔kəmˈponənt〕n. 零件
telecommunication〔͵tɛləkə͵mjunəˈkeʃən〕n. 電信
unnatural〔ʌnˈnætʃərəl〕adj. 不合情理的；不自然的
obstruction〔əbˈstrʌkʃən〕n. 阻礙
artificial〔͵ɑrtəˈfɪʃəl〕adj. 人為的
curb〔kɝb〕n. 抑制；約束

英文報紙必備國貿用語

◇ international trade 國際貿易

◇ export trade 出口貿易　　import trade 入口貿易

◇ unilateral trade 單邊貿易

◇ bilateral trade ; two-way trade 雙邊貿易

◇ multilateral trade 多邊貿易

◇ protectionism〔prə'tɛkʃənɪzm〕n. 貿易保護主義

◇ quota〔'kwotə〕n.（生產、進出口等的）配額

◇ agent〔'edʒənt〕n. 代理商

◇ exclusive distributor 總代理

◇ agreement〔ə'grimənt〕n. 合同；契約

◇ contract〔'kɑntrækt〕n. 契約

◇ installment〔ɪn'stɔlmənt〕n. 分期付款

◇ total price 總價　　buying rate 買價

◇ selling rate 賣價　　margin money 保證金

◇ mortgage〔'mɔrgɪdʒ〕n. 不動產抵押

◇ payment of duty 報關　　net weight 淨重

◇ commodity price 物價　　purchase〔'pɜtʃəs〕v. 購買

◇ wholesale〔'hol,sel〕n. 批發

◇ order〔'ɔrdɚ〕v. 訂購　　market〔'mɑrkɪt〕n. 市場

◇ outlet〔'aʊt,lɛt〕n. 銷路　　retail〔'ritel〕n. 零售

◇ slack season ; off season 淡季

◊ peak season 旺季　　chicken feed 小生意

◊ great deal 大買賣　　purchasing power 購買力

◊ conjuncture〔kən'dʒʌŋktʃə〕*n.* 時機

◊ only（fixed）price 不二價

◊ special price 特價　　reduced price 減價

◊ regular price 原價　　market price 市價

◊ discount〔'dɪskaʊnt〕*n.* 折扣

◊ horizontal competition 同業競爭

◊ cut-throat competition；blind competition 惡性競爭

◊ depreciation〔dɪ,priʃɪ'eʃən〕*n.* 貶值

◊ appreciation〔ə,priʃɪ'eʃən〕*n.* 升值

◊ oil producing nation(s) 產油國

◊ oil consuming nation(s) 石油消費國

◊ uniform invoice 統一發票　　exempt〔ɪg'zɛmpt〕*v.* 免稅

◊ evasion of duty（tax）逃稅

◊ entrance fee 入港手續費

◊ duty-free〔'djutɪ'fri〕*adj.* 免稅的

◊ accommodation〔ə,kɑmə'deʃən〕*n.* 貸款；融通

◊ associate〔ə'soʃɪ,et〕*n.* 合夥人

◊ bonus〔'bonəs〕*n.* 紅利；獎金　　cable〔'kebḷ〕*n.* 電報

◊ hypothecation〔haɪ,pɑθə'keʃən〕*n.* 押滙；抵押

◊ monopoly〔mə'nɑpḷɪ〕*n.* 壟斷

Jewelry   *Wednesday Jan. 5*

Gold is a girl's best friend at bonus time

How to spend your yearly bonus? Gold or crystal jewelry may be the perfect present for you or your beloved, a local newspaper reported yesterday.

Many jewelers have specially designed new pieces to appeal to couples.

Pendants engraved with phrases such as "true as gold" and "love is beautiful" were favored by lovers, the paper reported. Chains weighing about six grams

and costing about $2,600, and pendants were the most popular choices with buyers.

Crystal rings, earrings and brooches in classic French designs were also popular with women. Part of the appeal of crystal is that it only needs to be polished with a piece of velvet to keep its luster.

The average cost of each piece was between $2,000 and $7,000.

解答 ☞ p.266

1. Many jewelers have
   (A) stocked gold and crystal jewelry for the new year.
   (B) advertized jewelry for you and your beloved.
   (C) come up with plans for your yearly bonus.
   (D) come up with items particularly attractive for couples.

2. What is part of the appeal of crystal?
   (A) its popularity with women
   (B) its price
   (C) the ease with which it can be kept sparkling
   (D) its classic French design in rings, earings, and brooches

3. How can the jewelry best be described?
   (A) bulbous
   (B) necklaces
   (C) gleaming
   (D) brooches

黃金是女子的佳友

年終獎金該怎麼花呢？昨日一家地方報紙報導，黃金或水晶珠寶，可能是送給你自己或愛人的最佳禮物。

許多珠寶商爲了吸引情侶，特別設計了新的款式。

報導並指出，一些刻了名言的墜子，像「眞誠若金」、「愛即美好」深獲情人的偏愛。六克重，大約二千六百美元的鍊子或墜子，最受消費者歡迎。

典型法式設計的水晶戒指、耳環、以及胸針，也深受婦女的喜愛。水晶受歡迎，部分是因爲它只需要一塊絨布擦拭，便可保持它的光澤。

每件平均價格是在美金二千元到七千元之間。

** bonus〔'bonəs〕n. 獎賞；分紅
crystal〔'krɪstl̩〕n. 水晶
beloved〔bɪ'lʌvd〕n. 深愛的人
appeal〔ə'pil〕v. 投其所好　n. 吸引；魅力
pendant〔'pɛndənt〕n. 垂飾　engrave〔ɪn'grev〕v. 雕刻
phrase〔frez〕n. 片語；名言
brooch〔brotʃ, brutʃ〕n. 別針
velvet〔'vɛlvɪt〕n. 天鵝絨　luster〔'lʌstɚ〕n. 光澤

Fuel prices

Tuesday May 10

Higher taxes on gasoline proposed

The Economics Ministry has suggested that taxes on gasoline, diesel and kerosene products be raised in the next six months to offset revenue losses due to lower world crude oil prices.

Vice Economics Minister Yang Shi-chien said the ministry had proposed that the tax on gasoline be raised from 75 percent to 82 percent, and that on diesel and kerosene be increased from 60 percent to 65 percent.

The proposed tax hike needs to be approved by the Finance Ministry and then by the Executive Yuan.

"Our fuel prices are lower than our neighboring countries. We also have to consider the social costs of using fuels," he said.

"Besides, we are not an oil-producing country and should not sustain low fuel costs," he added.

Gasoline in Japan costs $35 per liter, in South Korea $22, in Hong Kong $20 and in Singapore, $19. It is $16 a liter Taiwan.

解答 ☞ p.266

1. What should happen because of lost revenue due to lower crude oil prices?

  (A) Revenue should be made up by increasing taxes on oil products.
  (B) Prices on oil products will go up.
  (C) More crude oil should be imported to offset the loss.
  (D) Taxes should be raised for six months.

2. What is a tax "hike"?

  (A) a deferment of taxation (B) an increase in taxation
  (C) a loss of tax revenue (D) an indexing of taxation

3. Consider the "social costs" of using fuels probably means

  (A) How much society can afford to pay for fuel is very important.
  (B) Fuel also has negative effects on society.
  (C) The advantages of cheap fuel have to be compared with its financial and other costs to the nation.
  (D) Cheap fuel has many benefits which might disappear if the price were raised.

4. Why shouldn't Taiwan sustain low fuel costs?

  (A) A lot of revenue could be earned through higher taxes on fuel.
  (B) It is not an oil-producing country and should discourage use of fuel.
  (C) It is not an oil-producing country and should encourage use of fuel.
  (D) Fuel prices will inevitably rise costing Taiwan much more.

計劃提高燃料稅

經濟部提議將在六個月內提高汽油、柴油及煤油製品的課稅，以平衡因世界原油價格的下跌所減少的稅收。

經濟部政務次長楊世緘指出，經濟部計劃汽油稅從百分之七十五提高到百分之八十二；而柴油稅和煤油稅從百分之六十增加到百分之六十五。

這項調稅方案須經過財政部，再經過行政院的同意。

他表示：「我們的燃料價格比鄰近幾個國家更低，我們也必須考慮到使用燃料時，所花費的社會成本。」

他並指出：「此外，我們國家並非產油國，不應該持續低價格的燃料費制。」

在日本，汽油每公升三十五美元，南韓每公升二十二美元，香港每公升二十美元，新加坡每公升十九美元，而台灣是每公升十六美元。

** gasoline〔'gæsə,lin〕n. 汽油
   propose〔prə'poz〕v. 計畫；策畫
   ministry〔'mɪnɪstrɪ〕n. 部   diesel〔'dizl〕n. 柴油
   kerosene〔'kɛrə,sin〕n. 煤油
   offset〔'ɔf,sɛt〕n. 抵消（物）
   revenue〔'rɛvə,nju〕n. 稅收   **due to** 因爲
   crude oil 原油   vice〔vaɪs〕n. 副…
   minister〔'mɪnɪstə〕n. 部長   hike〔haɪk〕n. 上漲
   Executive Yuan 行政院   fuel〔'fjuəl〕n. 燃料
   sustain〔sə'sten〕v. 持續   liter〔'litə〕n. 公升

Saturday Jan. 8

Trust companies did well in 1993

Compiled by The China Post

Local trust companies performed very well last year, with four firms achieving NT$1 billion (US$37.59 million) in pre-tax profits and one company earning over NT$1.5 billion, the Economic Daily News reported.

The Overseas Trust Corporation earned NT$1.5 billion(US$56.39 million). Employees shared nearly NT$10 million (US$ 375,940) of the new profits they helped to create, the report said.

Cathay, Taiwan First, China United Trust and Asia Trust each registered NT$1 billion (US$37.59 million)in profits. Asia Trust and Investment, whose stock listed capital was posted only at NT$1.6 billion(US$60.15 million), obviously was the best performing firm because it created nearly an NT$6 profit for each individual share.

On the other hand, Cathay, whose profits also amounted to NT$10 billion (US$ 375.94 million), could only add about NT$ 1 to each individual share. Its performance even fell behind that of Taiwan First and China United, which both had smaller amounts of capital.

解答☞ p.266

1. What does pre-tax mean?
   (A) before dividend payment
   (B) allowing for losses
   (C) after tax deductions
   (D) before tax deductions

2. Employees at the Overseas Trust Corporation
   (A) were given substantial salary rises.
   (B) were given bonuses from the profits made.
   (C) were given NT$10 million worth of shares.
   (D) were given employment bonuses.

3. According to the article, which is the best way to measure performance?
   (A) pre-tax profits
   (B) net capitalization
   (C) earnings per share
   (D) employee share bonus

4. Although Cathay registered large profits, why did its performance fall behind other firms?
   (A) Its share price had fallen.
   (B) It had a larger number of employees.
   (C) Its added value was less because of higher capitalization.
   (D) Its performance had declined from the previous year.

信託公司'93年表現優異

〔中國郵報〕經濟日報指出，地方信託公司去年表現良好，有四家公司除稅前的毛利達台幣十億元（美元三千七百五十九萬元），且有一家公司賺得十五億元以上。

報導並指出，海外的信託公司淨賺台幣十五億元（美金五千六百三十九萬元）。員工分享了將近台幣一千萬元（美金三十七萬五千九百四十元），這新的利潤也就是他們所協助創造出來的。

國泰、台灣第一、中國聯合，以及亞洲信託，各申報了台幣十億元（美金三千七百五十九萬元）的利潤。亞洲信託和投資公司的股市行情表的資金只有台幣十六億元（美金六千零十五萬元），顯然是表現最佳的公司，因為它在個人分攤利益創造了近台幣六元的利潤。

另一方面，國泰雖已達到台幣一百億元（美金三億七千五百九十四億元），卻只能增加大約台幣一元的個人分攤利益。它的表現甚至在台灣第一和中國聯合之後，因為他們的資本都較少。

** *pre-tax profit* 除稅前的毛利

 overseas〔ˌovəˈsiz〕*adj.* 海外的

 corporation〔ˌkɔrpəˈreʃən〕*n.* 股份公司

 employee〔ˌɪmˈplɔɪˈi〕*n.* 雇員

 register〔ˈrɛdʒɪstə〕*v.* 記錄；申報

Markets

Gold, dollar lower

Associated Press

London, Aug. 24 — The U.S. dollar was lower against other major currencies except the British pound in early European trading Tuesday. Gold prices were lower.

In Tokyo, the dollar closed at 103.97 yen, up 0.62 yen from Monday's close. Later in London, the dollar was quoted at 103.70 yen.

In London, the British pound was quoted at US$1.4980, down from US$1.5020 late Monday.

London's major bullion dealers fixed a recommended gold price of US$372.75 per ounce at midmorning, down from US$ 374.15 bid per ounce late Monday.

In Zurich, the bid price was US$ 372.75, down from US$373.90 late Monday.

In Hong Kong, gold fell US$1.08 to close at a bid US$372.27.

Silver traded in London at US$4.76 a troy ounce, down from US$4.80 a troy ounce Monday.

解答 ☞ p.266

1. What is this article about?

   (A) raw materials and commodities

   (B) technology and military matters

   (C) current events

   (D) currency and finance

2. From this article we can see that prices are constantly

   (A) deviating.

   (B) fluctuating.

   (C) bidding.

   (D) perverse.

FOCUS

● 各國貨幣

NT dollar (New Taiwan dollar) 新台幣

dollar〔'dɑlə〕*n.* 元（美國、加拿大的貨幣單位）

pound〔paʊnd〕*n.* 鎊（英國貨幣單位）

franc〔'fræŋk〕*n.* 法郎（法國、比利時的貨幣單位）

mark〔mɑrk〕*n.* 馬克（德國貨幣單位）

yen〔jɛn〕*n.* 圓（日本貨幣單位）

lira〔'lirɑ〕*n.* 里拉（義大利、土耳其貨幣單位）

rouble〔'rubl̩〕*n.* 盧布（俄羅斯貨幣單位）

金價、美元下跌

〔美聯社〕倫敦，八月二十四日電── 週四稍早的歐洲貨幣交易中，美元對其它主要貨幣的滙率，除英磅外，呈下跌走勢；金價亦隨之下跌。

東京滙市收盤價為一美元對一百零三點九七日圓，比星期一收盤時漲了零點六二日圓。稍後倫敦喊價到一美元對一百零三點七〇日圓。

在倫敦，英磅則叫價一英磅對一點四九八〇美元，比星期一的一英磅對一點五〇二〇美元為低。

倫敦主要的黃金交易商上午建議，將黃金公定價訂為每盎斯三百七十二點七五美元，較星期一每盎斯叫價三百七十四點一五美元下跌。

在蘇黎世，黃金公定價為三百七十二點七五美元，同樣比星期一的三百七十三點九〇美元下跌。

香港金市收盤時下跌一點〇八美元，以三百七十二點二七美元坐收。

倫敦銀塊交易自星期一的每盎斯四點八〇美元下跌至四點七六美元。

** currency〔ˋkɝənsɪ〕*n.* 通貨；貨幣　　quote〔kwot〕*v.* 喊價
bullion〔ˋbʊljən〕*n.* 金塊；銀塊
recommend〔͵rɛkəˋmɛnd〕*v.* 建議
bid〔bɪd〕*v.* 叫價；命令　　ounce〔aʊns〕*n.* 盎司
Zurich〔ˋzʊrɪk, ˋzɪʊrɪk〕*n.* 蘇黎世

U.S./Japan

Trade war discounted by U.S.

U.S. Secretary of State Warren Christopher has expressed confidence that political skirmishing between the United States and Japan would not escalate into a full-scale trade war.

He said the U.S. relationship with Japan was broad and healthy, marked by excellent military and diplomatic cooperation. But Japan's ever growing trade surplus with the United States, now around US $ 60 billion a year, needed urgent correction.

The measure was widely seen as aimed at Japan, following the failure last month of Clinton's summit with Japanese Prime Minister Morihiro Hosokawa. The leaders proved unable to agree on concrete moves to curb the Japanese surplus and open Japanese markets to U.S. goods and services.

解答 ☞ p. 266

1. What opinion did the U.S. Secretary of State express?
   (A) concern about skirmishes between the U.S. and Japan
   (B) his satisfaction with the U.S./Japan relationship
   (C) his hopes for escalation between the two countries
   (D) his expectation that there would be no escalation over trade

2. How did the Secretary describe the two nations' relations?
   (A) healthy but narrow
   (B) good apart from the unacceptable trade surplus with Japan
   (C) harmed by trade disputes and skirmishes
   (D) in urgent need of correction

3. What were the two nations' leaders unable to achieve at the summit?
   (A) an agreement on steps to open Japan's market to U.S. goods and services
   (B) an agreement on the size of increase of the Japanese trade surplus
   (C) an agreement to increase trade between the two nations
   (D) an agreement to limit Japanese exports

美日不會有貿易戰

美國國務卿克里斯多福自信地表示，美日的政治衝突不會擴大爲全面性的貿易戰。

他說，就良好的軍事及外交合作來看，美日兩國的關係廣泛且健全。但是，日本對美國的貿易出超不斷成長，現在已高達每年六百億美元，這確實急需調整。

上個月，柯林頓總統與日本首相細川護熙高峯會談判失敗，因此，超級三○一條款的恢復一般認爲是衝著日本來的。兩國領袖皆無法採取具體行動，來抑制日對美的出超與開放美國貨品及服務業至日本市場。

** discount〔'dɪskaʊnt,dɪs'kaʊnt〕v. 打折
   U.S. Secretary of State 美國國務卿
   skirmishing〔'skɜmɪʃɪŋ〕n. 小衝突
   escalate〔'ɛskə,let〕v. 逐漸擴大
   full-scale〔'fʊl'skel〕adj. 全面的
   diplomatic〔,dɪplə'mætɪk〕adj. 外交的
   surplus〔'sɜpləs〕n. 餘額
   summit〔'sʌmɪt〕n. 高峯會
   Prime Minister 首相
   concrete〔kɑn'krit,'kɑnkrit〕adj. 具體的
   curb〔kɜb〕v. 抑制

Part 7

Editorial & Commentary 社論專欄

Drug

Deal with the drug problem

It seems that drug traffickers are more ingenious than most of us might think. Recently a drug trafficking ring tried to smuggle heroin into Taiwan by putting the drug in gloves and having people swallow them and bring the contraband in.

The fact that these men would risk their lives and imprisonment for a modest sum of money is a reflection of the wide-spread greed on this island.

The government must map out a comprehensive program to eliminate drug abuse and trafficking. Increased police investigation and stricter Customs inspections must be included in the program.

More important are efforts to reduce the demand for drugs. When the demand declines the supply will decrease. The movement to help addicts kick the habit and to prevent others from becoming addicts must be stepped up.

解答☞ p. 266

1. According to a report, drug traffickers tried to smuggle heroin into Taiwan by
   (A) putting it in their jeans.
   (B) wearing gloves filled with the drug.
   (C) having rings made that were filled with the drug.
   (D) putting the drug in gloves and having people swallow them.

2. The government should eliminate drug abuse and trafficking by
   (A) increasing the demand for drugs.
   (B) decreased police investigations.
   (C) infrequent customs inspections.
   (D) increased police investigations and customs inspections.

Focus

法務部長馬英九最近指出，爲了遏制毒品走私，死刑是必要的手段，因爲「對抗毒品的第一步就是斷其來源。」

對付毒品問題

毒販似乎比我們所能想像的還要天才。最近，有販毒集團為了要走私海洛英到台灣，而將毒品裝入手套中並讓人吞下，然後將這些毒品帶進來。

這些人為了為數不多的錢，寧願冒生命及作牢的危險，這項事實正顯示出瀰漫全島的貪婪之風。

政府必須擬定一套完善的方案來消除吸毒及販毒。此一方案必須包括增加警方調查，及加強海關更嚴格的檢查。

更重要的是要努力降低對毒品的需求。當需求降低，供應也會相對的減少。此外必須採取行動，幫助吸毒者戒除毒癮，並防止其他人染上毒癮。

** trafficker〔ˈtræfɪkɚ〕n. 交易者
ingenious〔ɪnˈdʒinjəs〕adj. 天才的
smuggle〔ˈsmʌgl〕v. 走私　　heroin〔ˈhɛro·ɪn〕n. 海洛英
contraband〔ˈkɑntrəˌbænd〕n. 走私貨　　**map out** 擬定
comprehensive〔ˌkɑmprɪˈhɛnsɪv〕adj. 完整的
eliminate〔ɪˈlɪməˌnet〕v. 消除
addict〔ˈædɪkt〕n. 對～有癮的人　　**step up** 增進；加強

Commentary

Monday Nov. 8

Spend more on the arts

Although the Council for Cultural Planning and Development has drawn up a draft for a law to govern the establishment of a national cultural and art foundation, the bill is gathering dust in the Legislative Yuan.

With their incomes greatly increased, local residents can now afford almost every kind of luxury as well as all daily necessities. The affluence of the people is unparalleled in Chinese history.

Increased prosperity has led to materialistic tendencies, especially among the younger generation. Obsession with material possessions makes many people pursue wealth endlessly and aggressively and drives some to engage in illegal activities.

Our soecity should rediscover the important role that culture and art play in generating real happiness and contentment. Instead of being preoccupied exclusively with economic and materialistic pursuits, Taiwan residents should pay more attention to spiritual welfare. An interest in art, music and books is crucial for happiness.

解答☞ p. 266

1. In the newspaper's opinion, the younger generation
   (A) is obsessed with material possessions.
   (B) drives too aggressively.
   (C) is poorer than any other generation in Chinese history.
   (D) is too lazy.

2. The author believes that Taiwan residents should
   (A) pay more attention to spiritual welfare.
   (B) pay more money to churches.
   (C) pay more for music and books.
   (D) be content with material possessions.

多花點經費於藝術上

雖然文建會已擬出草案，要設置國家文化藝術基金會，但立法院卻遲遲未審核此法案。

由於收入大幅增加，現在，本地居民不但有能力買所有的日用品，也有能力買各種奢侈品。此地人民的富裕，是中國歷史上前所未見的。

高度的繁榮造成了物質傾向，年輕人尤其如此。追求物質的慾望，使許多人無休止地汲汲追求財富，並驅使某些人從事非法勾當。

文化藝術能產生真正的快樂和滿足，我們的社會應重新了解其所扮演的重要角色。台灣的居民不應將過多的心力，投注於經濟和物質的追求，而應更重視精神上的財富。想要快樂，培養對藝術、音樂及書本的興趣，是很重要的。

** the Council for Cultural Planning and Development（*CCPD*）
文化建設發展委員會

foundation〔faʊnˈdeʃən〕*n.* 基金會　Legislative Yuan 立法院

luxury〔ˈlʌkʃərɪ〕*n.* 奢侈（品）

unparalleled〔ʌnˈpærə‚lɛld〕*adj.* 無比的

obsession〔əbˈsɛʃən〕*n.* 慾望

aggressively〔əˈgrɛsɪvlɪ〕*adv.* 積極地

contentment〔kənˈtɛntmənt〕*n.* 滿足

preoccupy〔priˈɑkjə‚paɪ〕*v.* 使全神貫注

pursuit〔pəˈsut〕*n.* 追求　crucial〔ˈkruʃəl〕*adj.* 極重要的

UFO

UFO sighters not nuts

People who see flying saucers are not nuts, and neither are folks who claim to hitch rides with extraterrestrials, researchers say.

Spanos said the only significant difference between the UFO sighters and the others was that those who reported flying saucers had previously established belief in the existence of UFOs and in aliens.

"Some UFO reports are likely to occur when external events are ambiguous or unfamiliar, when darkness makes it hard to see clearly or when one is in that disoriented state just before falling asleep," the study said.

解答 ☞ p. 266

■ What is one of the important reasons why the sighters' information may not be considered to be reliable?

(A) They were all white collar.

(B) They were already of the belief that UFOs exist.

(C) Only 20% of the encounters reported occured during the day.

(D) They were no different from the control group.

聲稱看過飛碟的人不是瘋子

研究人員指出，看到飛碟的人不是瘋子，那些聲稱和外星人搭乘飛碟旅行的人也不是。

史班諾指出，看過幽浮的人，和其他人唯一不同的地方，就是聲稱看過飛碟的人，相信幽浮和外星人的存在。

研究指出，「有些人看到幽浮，可能是因為當時外在環境模糊不清、或很陌生，或是因為黑暗使人難以看清楚，也可能是因為當事人處於入睡前神智不清的狀態。」

** UFO 幽浮；不明飛行物體（ *unidentified flying object* ）
　　nut〔nʌt〕 *n*. 瘋子　　　*flying saucer* 飛碟
　　hitch a ride 搭便車旅行
　　extraterrestrials〔͵ɛkstrətəˈrɛstrɪəlz〕 *n*. 地球以外的人
　　alien〔ˈeljən〕 *n*. 外星人；外國人　external〔ɪkˈstɜnl〕 *adj*. 外在的
　　ambiguous〔æmˈbɪgjuəs〕 *adj*. 含糊的
　　disoriented〔dɪsˈorɪ͵ɛntɪd〕 *adj*. 分不清方向的

Focus

　　加拿大渥太華卡里頓大學的史班諾博士表示，那些宣稱看過幽浮的人多半是中產階級的白領人士，受過相當高的教育。在智力、幻想傾向、及受暗示支配性方面，和常人沒有兩樣。

Handicapped need better educational opportunities

Statistics from a recent survey indicate that in Taiwan one out of every 25 school children is handicapped and that the vast majority of the handicapped children do not get the education they need. This is a disgrace considering the affluence of Taiwan and the government's claim that welfare for the handicapped is high on its list of priorities.

Most of the handicapped denied the opportunity for sufficient education have the ability to learn. The reason they are not properly educated is that there are not enough educational facilities specially designed for them.

The central and local governments should allocate more funds to the creation of such facilities. Schools for the mentally handicapped, in particular, should be increased, for these are the individuals whose lives can improve the most with what the training schools can provide.

解答 ☞ p.266

1. Statistics show that
   (A) 25 school children are handicapped.
   (B) Taiwanese children aren't getting the education they need.
   (C) Taiwanese children hate school.
   (D) One in 25 school children is handicapped.

2. Handicapped children don't receive the education they need because
   (A) the government doesn't have the money to spend on education.
   (B) welfare for the handicapped is not high on the government's list of priorities.
   (C) they don't want to go to school.
   (D) there are not enough educational facilities for them.

3. The number of special educational facilities should be increased so
   (A) classes won't be crowded.
   (B) children won't have to travel so far to school.
   (C) there would be more jobs for teachers.
   (D) children who are handicapped can improve their lives.

殘障者需要更好的教育機會

最近一項調查統計資料顯示：台灣每二十五位學童中，就有一位殘障，而且大多數的殘障兒童得不到他們所需要的教育。就台灣富裕的程度，以及政府一再聲明會優先考慮殘障人士福利等情況來看，這真是一種恥辱。

許多無法獲得充分教育機會的殘障人士，是具有學習能力的。他們無法正常的受教育，主要是因為特別為他們而設計的教育設施不敷使用。

中央與地方政府應該要撥更多的預算來建設這些設施。尤其要增加啟智學校的興建，因為有了學校所提供的訓練，他們的生活便能獲得極大的改善。

** handicapped〔ˈhændɪˌkæpt〕*adj*. 殘障的
statistics〔stəˈtɪstɪks〕*n.pl*. 統計資料　survey〔ˈsɚve〕*n*. 調查
vast〔væst〕*adj*. 巨大的　majority〔məˈdʒɔrətɪ〕*n*. 大多數
disgrace〔dɪsˈgres〕*n*. 恥辱　considering〔kənˈsɪdərɪŋ〕*prep*. 就…而論
affluence〔ˈæfluəns〕*n*. 富裕　claim〔klem〕*v*. 宣稱
priority〔praɪˈɔrətɪ〕*n*. 優先的事物　deny〔dɪˈnaɪ〕*v*. 不給予
facilities〔fəˈsɪlətɪz〕*n.pl*. 設施
allocate〔ˈæləˌket〕*v*. 把…撥給~　fund〔fʌnd〕*n*. 資金

英文報紙必備教育用語

◇ academy〔ə'kædəmɪ〕n. 學院　National school 國立學校
◇ provincial school 省立學校　municipal school 市立學校
◇ district school 縣立學校　public school 公立學校
◇ private school 私立學校
◇ supplementary school;"cram" school 補習班
◇ professor〔prə'fɛsə〕n. 教授　full-time professor 專任教授
◇ adjunct professor 兼任教授　lecturer〔'lɛktʃərə〕n. 講師
◇ assistant〔ə'sɪstənt〕n. 助教

◇ registration〔,rɛdʒɪ'streʃən〕n. 登記；註冊
◇ Joint College Entrance Examination（JCEE）大學聯考
◇ oral examination 口試　written examination 筆試
◇ pass〔pæs, pɑs〕v. 及格　semester〔sə'mɛstə〕n. 學期
◇ academic year 學年　dormitory〔'dɔrmə,torɪ〕n. 宿舍
◇ credit〔'krɛdɪt〕n. 學分

◇ freshman〔'frɛʃmən〕n. 大一學生
◇ sophomore〔'sɑfm̩,or, -,ɔr〕n. 大二學生
◇ junior〔'dʒunjə〕n. 大三學生　senior〔'sinjə〕n. 大四學生
◇ graduate student 研究生　overseas student 留學生
◇ ba elor〔'bætʃələ〕n.（BA）學士
◇ master〔'mæstə, 'mɑs-〕n.（MA）碩士
◇ doctor〔'dɑktə〕n. 博士

Wednesday Jan. 26

Travelers beware

The news that at least five tourists from Taiwan were killed in Thailand has shocked the public at home and has warned them of the potential danger involving foreign travel.

The hair-raising news hit home while foreign travel is becoming a fad here. Thailand is among the favorite tourist spots because of its low cost of living. Now the travelers are worried about their safety and they need information on how to avoid danger while visiting foreign lands.

One bit of advice was offered by the Taipei Travel Business Association, which cautioned travelers against frequenting troubled spots in unsafe places, especially backward locales in Southeast Asia and mainland China.

The travelers should avoid high-risk areas. Such lists should be provided by government authorities in charge of tourism to alert the travelers of the potential danger involved.

解答 ☞ p.266

1. What has the news warned the Taiwanese public of ?
   (A) possible danger in traveling abroad
   (B) the danger of being Chinese in Thailand
   (C) murders that will happen in Thailand
   (D) the danger of trusting police abroad

2. What advice was given to travelers by the Travel Business Association ?
   (A) Travelers should avoid areas with a low standard of living.
   (B) Travelers should avoid knowing tourist spots if possible.
   (C) Travelers should avoid government authorities in backward areas.
   (D) Travelers should try to avoid backward areas in countries they visit.

旅客小心

至少有五位來自台灣的旅客在泰國被殺害，這項消息震驚了本地民衆，也警告人民去海外旅遊帶來的潛在危機。

到國外旅遊已成了此地風尙，然而，這項令人驚駭的消息卻震懾了全台灣。泰國因低廉的物價，而成了觀光客的最愛之一。現在，旅客們擔心自身的安全，同時，遊覽國外時，也需要足夠的資訊以避免危險。

台灣觀光協會提供了一點建議，警告旅客不要前往危險地區內，治安混亂的地區，尤其是東南亞及中國大陸的落後地區。

旅客應避免前往高危險地區。負責旅遊業的有關當局，也應列出這些地區的名單，讓旅客留心其潛在的危機。

** beware 〔bɪ'wɛr〕 v. 小心　　tourist 〔'tʊrɪst〕 n. 遊客
Thailand 〔'taɪlənd〕 n. 泰國　　potential 〔pə'tɛnʃəl〕 adj. 潛在的
hair-raising 〔'hɛr,rezɪŋ〕 adj. 令人毛骨悚然的
fad 〔fæd〕 n. 流行　　　　spot 〔spɑt〕 n. 地點
Taipei Travel Business Association　台灣觀光協會
caution 〔'kɔʃən〕 v. 警告　　backward 〔'bækwəd〕 adj. 落後的
locale 〔lo'kæl , -'kɑl〕 n. 現場
high-risk 〔'haɪ'rɪsk〕 adj. 高危險的
authority 〔ə'θɔrɛtɪ〕 n. 當局　　tourism 〔'tʊrɪzm〕 n. 旅遊業
alert 〔ə'lɝt〕 v. 留心

Editorial

Friday Mar. 11

Delay of arms purchase a wise decision

Arms purchases in this country have been conducted by the military in secrecy for national security reasons, with little or no supervision by the Legislative Yuan. Yin's case has exposed the many problems that have come to a head after decades of negligence.

Against this backdrop, it is a wise decision that the government has decided to delay the purchase of weapons from the United States, including US$188-million worth of M-60 tanks, two squadrons of T-38 trainer jets, and Modified Air Defense batteries valued at a reported US$1 billion.

The decision is certainly wise considering the growing skepticism about the process of Taiwan's arms acquisition and the long shadow cast by Captain Yin's murder. It is also prudent considering the budgetary constraints and questionable technical capabilities of the weapons under consideration for acquisition.

解答☞p.266

1. Arms purchases in Taiwan occur in secrecy because
   (A) newspaper won't publish any details.
   (B) of national security reasons.
   (C) no one is interested in being involved.
   (D) the Legislative Yuan doesn't have time to supervise the deals.

2. The government has decided to
   (A) purchase weapons from the US.
   (B) allow newspapers to print all details about arms deals.
   (C) spend US$188 million on weapons.
   (D) delay purchasing weapons from the US.

FOCUS

這批武器採購，代號為「陸鵬專案」，其中
攻擊直昇機採購四十二架。自八十二年起分五年
交機：第一年八架，第二年九架，第三年九架，
第四、五年各八架。

延緩軍購是明智的決定

　　由於顧及國家安全，國內的武器採購一直由軍中秘密指揮，而立法院很少監督。在幾十年的疏忽後，尹清楓命案使問題臻於白熱化。

　　就此背景來看，政府延緩向美採購武器的決定是明智的。這批武器包括價值一億八千八百萬美元的M-60型坦克，兩個中隊的T-38教練噴射機，及據報導為10億元的改良型地對空列砲。

　　台灣的軍購過程令人質疑，而且尹上校命案造成了長期的陰影，就此情況來看，政府的決定，無疑是明智的。而且…若考慮到預算的緊縮，以及大眾對武器性能的質疑等問題，這項決定其實是非常正確的。

** purchase〔'pɝtʃəs〕v. 購買　　　　conduct〔kən'dʌkt〕v. 指揮
in secrecy 秘密地　　　　　supervision〔ˌsupɚ'vɪʒən〕n. 監督
the Legislative Yuan 立法院　　　expose〔ɪk'spoz〕v. 暴露
negligence〔'nɛglədʒəns〕n. 疏忽
backdrop〔'bæk,drɑp〕n. 背景　　weapon〔'wɛpən〕n. 武器
squadron〔'skwɑdrən〕n. 空軍中隊　　jet〔dʒɛt〕n. 噴射機
modified〔'mɑdə,faɪd〕adj.改良的　battery〔'bætərɪ〕n. 列砲
skepticism〔'skɛptə,sɪzəm〕n. 懷疑
prudent〔'prudn̩t〕adj. 謹慎的；明智的
budgetary〔'bʌdʒɪ,tɛrɪ〕adj. 預算的
constraint〔kən'strent〕n. 拘束或限制之事物

Commentary   *Tuesday Dec. 20*

Stiffer penalties for drunk driving urgently needed

Drunk driving has become increasingly common over the past few years, according to news reports. It is time for the authorities to assume a truly tough stance toward this dangerous act.

In Taipei, the number of traffic accidents resulting from drunk driving increased from 1,123 in 1990 to 1,900 in 1991, and to 2,341 in 1992. So far this year more than 2,300 such accidents have occurred in the city.

In many countries, prison terms are imposed on those caught driving when drunk. Here on this island the maximum penalty is a fine — NT$5,400 (US$218). In addition, the legal limits on drunk driving are too lax: a driver is considered guilty of drunk driving if, when caught, he or she has more than 0.5 milligrams of alcohol in the bloodstream.

The traffic death toll on the island's roads can be greatly reduced if law enforcement against drunk driving is tightened.

解答 ☞ p.266

1. Traffic accidents resulting from drunk driving were reported to have increased from
   (A) 1,123 in 1990 to 2,300 in 1992.
   (B) 1,123 in 1990 to 2,341 in 1992.
   (C) 1,123 in 1990 to 1,900 in 1992.
   (D) 1,900 in 1990 to 2,341 in 1992.

2. It is believed that drunk drivers are treated
   (A) too leniently with light penalties.
   (B) harshly as laws are enforced strictly.
   (C) more severely in Taiwan than other countries.
   (D) badly as they have to pay large fines.

3. In Taiwan, the maximum drunk driving penalty is
   (A) a prison term.
   (B) a fine of more than $NT5,400.
   (C) confiscation of any alcohol the drivers has.
   (D) a fine of $NT5,400.

酒後開車需重罰

根據新聞報告顯示，近幾年來，酒後駕車愈來愈常見。現在是有關當局對此危險的行為，採取確切強硬態度的時候了。

在台北，因酒後駕車而引起交通事故的數目，一九九〇年為一千一百廿三件，一九九一年增為一千九百件，到一九九二年更增加為二千三百四十一件。台北市目前為止，此類事故已超過二千三百件。

在許多國家中，酒後開車被捕，免不了有牢獄之災。而在台灣，最重的懲罰也只罰款新台幣五千四百元(美金二百一十八元)。此外，對於酒後駕車的法律定義太過鬆弛：當駕駛人被攔截下來測試時，血管中要含有〇·五毫克以上的酒精，才算是酒後開車。

假如對於酒後駕車的懲罰能強制施行，那麼，在台灣，公路上的交通意外死亡事件便會大幅減少了。

** stiff〔stɪf〕*adj.* 硬的；嚴厲的　　penalty〔'pɛnl̩tɪ〕*n.* 刑罰
urgently〔'ɝdʒəntlɪ〕*adv.* 緊急地
authority〔ə'θɔrətɪ〕*n.* 當局　　assume〔ə'sjum〕*v.* 採取
stance〔stæns〕*n.* 態度　　impose〔ɪm'poz〕*v.* 加(懲罰)於
maximum〔'mæksəməm〕*n.* 極大值　　fine〔faɪn〕*n.* 罰金
milligram〔'mɪlə‚græm〕*n.* 毫克
alcohol〔'ælkə‚hɔl〕*n.* 酒
bloodstream〔'blʌd‚strim〕*n.* 血管中之血液

英文報紙必備交通用語

◇ traffic signs 交通號誌
◇ pavement〔'pevmənt〕n. 人行道
◇ avenue〔'ævə,nju〕n.（南北向）大街（東西向為 street）
◇ alley〔'ælɪ〕n. 小巷　　lane〔len〕n. 巷弄；小路
◇ one way street; single lane 單行道
◇ overpass〔'ovɚ,pæs〕n.; foot bridge 天橋
◇ underpass〔'ʌndɚ,pæs〕n. 地下道

◇ subway〔'sʌb,we〕n. 地下鐵　　toll station 收費站
◇ elevated road 高架道路
◇ automobile〔,ɔtə'mobɪl〕n. 汽車
◇ truck〔trʌk〕n. 卡車　　gravel truck 沙石車
◇ sedan〔sɪ'dæn〕n. 轎車　　compact car 小轎車
◇ jeep〔dʒip〕n. 吉普車

◇ regular gasoline 普通汽油
◇ premium gasoline; extra gasoline 高級汽油
◇ unleaded〔ʌn'lɛdɪd〕adj. 無鉛的（汽油）
◇ engine oil 機油　　number plate 牌照
◇ traffic volume 交通量　　rush hour 尖峯時間
◇ traffic regulations 交通規則　　traffic control 交通管制
◇ mass rapid transit system 大衆捷運系統
◇ traffic jam 交通阻塞

Editorial

Friday Feb. 25

Democracy takes yet another stride forward

Saturday's mayoral and county council elections marked still another step forward for the Republic of China in developing democracy on this island.

The ruling Kuomintang captured 254 of the 309 mayoral positions contested, or 82.2 percent of the total. The overwhelming majority indicates that the party has succeeded in maintaining its power base.

Even so, it is worthy of note that the KMT suffered a loss of 43 positions in the mayoral election while the opposition Democratic Progressive Party (DPP) captured 21 positions — 15 more than its current number of 6.

But the decline in the KMT's edge over the opposition, despite the ruling party's enormous resources, has a message that the party must not make light of. The message is that if the party wants to stay in power it must strive to meet the wishes and needs of the people. And to do this the party must be more careful to gauge public attitudes and sentiments.

解答☞p.266

1. Why did the mayoral and county elections mark a step
   forward for democracy on the island ?
   (A) The ruling KMT captured 82 percent of the vote.
   (B) The KMT retained its power base.
   (C) The DPP increased its power.
   (D) The positions were chosen on the basis of elections.

2. What do the results mean for the KMT ?
   (A) They still have the support of the majority of
   voters in Taiwan.
   (B) They can afford to be complacent with such a large
   majority.
   (C) The opposition is not worth worrying about.
   (D) The KMT has been gaining support in recent years.

3. What happened to the DPP in the election?
   (A) They failed to get their message across.
   (B) They did much worse than before.
   (C) They more than tripled their number of positions.
   (D) They suffered a loss of seats to the KMT.

4. The KMT shouldn't make light of
   (A) its enormous resources.
   (B) the DPP.
   (C) the world.
   (D) the opinions of the public.

台灣向民主邁進

週六的鄉鎮市長與縣議員選舉顯示，台灣再度向民主邁進一大步。

在三百零九席縣市長中，執政的國民黨占了二百五十四席，為總數的百分之八十二點二。這項壓倒性的勝利表示國民黨維持了其政權基礎。

即使如此，有件事值得注意。在鄉鎮市長選舉中，國民黨少了四十三席，而民進黨占了二十一席，比之前的六席多了十五席。

儘管執政黨具有強大的資產，但國民黨和反對黨的實力日趨接近，更不可忽略這項衰退所傳遞的信息：那就是，假如國民黨想繼續執政，就必須努力達成人民的願望和需求。因此，執政黨應該更小心地判斷民眾的態度和情緒。

✸✸ democracy 〔dəˈmɑkrəsɪ〕 *n.* 民主政體
stride 〔straɪd〕 *n.* 一大步　　mayoral 〔ˈmeɪrəl〕 *adj.* 市長的；鎮長的
council 〔ˈkaʊnsl̩〕 *n.* 議會
Kuomintang 〔ˈkwoˈmɪnˈtæŋ〕 *n.* 國民黨 (**KMT**)
contest 〔kənˈtɛst〕 *v.* 爭奪 (席位)
overwhelming 〔ˌovəˈhwɛlmɪŋ〕 *adj.* 壓倒性的
the opposition 反對黨；在野黨
Democratic Progressive Party (**DPP**) 民主進步黨
enormous 〔ɪˈnɔrməs〕 *adj.* 巨大的
make light of 輕視　　gauge 〔gedʒ〕 *v.* 判斷

Pitch in
to prevent crime

With the Chinese New Year just around the corner, a holiday spirit is in the air which will continue long after Lunar New Year's Day. While this is a time of exhilaration, it is also a time when crime and juvenile delinquency may pose a serious threat to lives and property.

Police have launched an anti-crime and public safety program to help ensure safety during this holiday season. Private citizens, besides police, should do their share in preventing criminal activity.

Stepped-up police action is immensely important at this time in reducing criminal behavior. But private citizens must pitch in and help. They should be more alert for illegal activity and report anyone or anything that looks suspect. And they should also refrain from engaging in wild merrymaking, which is harmful to health and may give would-be criminals the opportunity to carry out their evil designs.

解答☞ p.266

1. What is juvenile delinqency?
   (A) violent crime
   (B) crime against property
   (C) crimes committed by the young
   (D) careless behavior during the new year.

2. Citizens should refrain from
   (A) partying wildly.
   (B) cooperating with the police in their work.
   (C) pitching in and helping.
   (D) going out unnecessarily.

FOCUS

●犯罪相關字彙

abettor 〔əˈbɛtɚ〕 n. 敎唆犯
accessory 〔ækˈsɛsərɪ〕 n. 從犯
accomplice 〔əˈkɑmplɪs〕 n. 共犯
bail 〔bel〕 n. 保釋；保釋金
cache 〔kæʃ〕 n. (危險物)藏匿所

努力預防犯罪

農曆新年的脚步接近了，到處瀰漫著年節的氣氛，將一直持續到年後。這是令人愉悅的時刻。然而，在這段時間中，犯罪及青少年的不當行爲也嚴重地威脅我們的生命財產。

警方開始實行一項消滅犯罪及提倡公共安全的計劃，以確保假期中的治安。除了警方之外，老百姓們也該共同分擔預防犯罪活動。

此時警方的擴大行動對於降低犯罪行爲是非常重要的。但民衆們也必須努力和幫忙。對於犯罪活動應更加謹愼，看到可疑的人或物要報警。而且，要儘量避免狂歡，那不但傷身，又會爲那些想要犯罪的人製造機會，來完成其不法勾當。

** ***pitch in*** 開始拼命工作　exhilaration〔ɪg͵zɪlə'reʃən〕*n.* 高興
juvenile〔'dʒuvənl〕*adj.* 年輕的
delinquency〔dɪ'lɪŋkwənsɪ〕*n.* 不當行爲
launch〔lɔntʃ〕*v.* 開始　rampant〔'ræmpənt〕*adj.* 猖獗的
neglectful〔nɪ'glɛktfəl〕*adj.* 不注意的
stepped-up〔'stɛpt͵ʌp〕*adj.* 提高的
immensely〔ɪ'mɛnslɪ〕*adv.* 非常　alert〔ə'lɝt〕*adj.* 留心的
refrain〔rɪ'fren〕*v.* 抑制　engage〔ɪn'gedʒ〕*v.* 捲入
would-be〔'wʊd͵bi〕*adj.* 將要成爲～的
carry out 完成

Monday Mar. 28

Improve junior high school education

The Ministry of Education is planning to extend compulsory education for one year for junior high school students who do not plan to further their schooling by entering senior high school. These students will learn job skills for two years, beginning in the third year of junior high school. This move has been seen as an attempt to expand junior high school education.

The quality of junior high school education has received much criticism in recent years. Standards are so low at some junior high schools that their graduates do not know much more than graduates of elementary schools.

Educational authorities should work hard to improve the facilities, teacher qualifications and requirements at junior high schools.

Students in junior high school are still receiving their basic training. Unless they are well grounded in such basic skills as Chinese and mathematics, they will not benefit much from vocational training.

解答 ☞ p.266

1. The ministry of Education plans to
   (A) make education compulsory.
   (B) extend compulsory education for one year for junior high students.
   (C) allow students to drop out of junior high school.
   (D) force junior high students to find jobs.

2. Students who don't plan to attend senior high school will
   (A) have to find jobs immediately.
   (B) have to study Chinese and mathematics.
   (C) be able to choose the subjects they will study.
   (D) learn job skills for two years.

3. Education at junior high schools has been
   (A) praised because students know much more than elementary school graduates.
   (B) improved so standards are higher.
   (C) criticised because standards are low.
   (D) expanded so students can learn more.

4. In the newspapers' opinion, educational authorities should
   (A) commission architects to design better schools.
   (B) increase teachers' pay.
   (C) improve facilities, teacher qualifications and requirements.
   (D) lower the requirements for students.

改善國中教育

　　對於不打算入高中繼續升學的國中生，教育部計劃將其義務教育延長一年。這些學生將從國三起，學習二年的工作技巧。此舉被認為是延長國中教育的嘗試。

　　近年來，國中教育的素質倍受批評。有些國中水準很低，以致於它們的畢業生所知不見得比國小畢業生多。

　　教育當局應該努力改善國中的設備、師資及必需條件。

　　國中學生仍在接受基本訓練。除非他們的基本學科如國文和數學，都已打好了基礎，否則他們無法從職業訓練中獲益。

** the Ministry of Education 教育部
　　compulsory 〔kəm'pʌlsərɪ〕 *adj.* 義務性的
　　criticism 〔'krɪtə,sɪzəm〕 *n.* 批評
　　standard 〔'stændəd〕 *n.* 水準　　authority 〔ə'θɔrətɪ〕 *n.* 當局
　　facility 〔fə'sɪlətɪ〕 *n.* 設備
　　qualification 〔,kwɑləfə'keʃən〕 *n.* 資格
　　requirement 〔rɪ'kwaɪrmənt〕 *n.* 必要條件
　　be well grounded 根底好的

Part 8

看懂英文報紙必備常識

CLASSIFIED ADS
分類廣告必備用語

Travel ·········· 旅遊

◇ air fare　飛機票價
◇ reserve〔rɪˈzɝv〕*v.* 預訂 (房間)
◇ single room〔ˈsɪŋ]ˈrum〕*n.* 單人房
◇ double room〔ˈdʌb]ˈrum〕*n.* 雙人房
◇ twin room〔ˈtwɪnˈrum〕*n.* 雙床房
◇ suite〔swit〕*n.* 套房

ELLIOT TOURS
SPECIAL FARES
Los Angeles 14500
Bangkok　7800
HongKong　5000
Seoul　　　7300
VANCOUVER 20900

Appointments ········· 求才

◇ promotion〔prəˈmoʃən〕*n.* 升級；升職
◇ must〔mʌst〕*n.* 必需之事
◇ specialize〔ˈspɛʃəlˌaɪz〕*v.* 專攻
◇ résumé〔ˌrɛzjuˈme〕*n.* ；
　curriculum vitae ("C.V.") 履歷表
◇ negotiable〔nɪˈgoʃɪəb]〕*adj.* 可商議的
◇ contract〔ˈkɑntrækt〕*n.* 合約

WANTED
International Travel/
Adventure Club has job
opening in Sales/Promotion
Fluency in Mandarin a must
Please Call Tom Lin

Personals ········· 小啓

◇ pen pal　筆友　　　◇ mature〔məˈtjʊr〕*adj.* 成熟的
◇ correspond〔ˌkɔrəˈspɑnd〕*v.* (與人)通信
◇ response〔rɪˈspɑns〕*n.* 回覆

Education ········· 教育

◇ visa extension 簽證期延長

◇ working permit 工作許可證

◇ resident visa 居住簽證 (一年)

◇ departure / re-entry 出境 / 再入境

◇ institute 〔'ɪnstə,tjut 〕 *n.*

學會；語言研習班

◇ certificate 〔sə'tɪfəkɪt 〕 *n.* 證書

◇ flexible 〔'flɛksəbl 〕 *adj.* 可變通的

◇ schedule 〔'skɛdʒʊl 〕 *n.* 行程表

◇ bilingual 〔baɪ'lɪŋgwəl 〕 *adj.* 用兩種語言的

 ## Car for rent ········· 租車

◇ mileage 〔'maɪlɪdʒ〕 *n.* 行駛哩數；耗油量

◇ brochure 〔 bro'ʃur 〕 *n.* 小冊子

◇ cordial 〔'kɔrdʒəl〕 *adj.* 熱誠的　full insurance coverage 全險

 ## House for rent ········· 租房子

◇ realty 〔'rɪəltɪ〕 *n.* 不動產　ping 〔pɪŋ〕 *n.* 坪

◇ panoramic 〔,pænə'ræmɪk〕 *adj.* 視野遼濶的

◇ utility 〔ju'tɪlətɪ〕 *n.* 水、電、瓦斯費

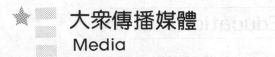

大衆傳播媒體
Media

I. *News Agencies* 新聞通訊社

- Agence France Press（*AFP*）　　法新社〔法〕
- Associated Press（*AP*）　　　　美聯社〔美〕
- Pan-Asia Newspaper Alliance　　泛亞通訊社〔日〕
  （*PANA*）
- Reuters　　　　　　　　　　　　路透社〔英〕
- United Press International（*UPI*）合衆國際社〔美〕
- Central News Agency（*CNA*）　中央通訊社〔中〕
- Liberty News Agency（*LNA*）　自由新聞社〔中〕
- Xinhua News Agency（*XNA*）　新華社〔中共〕

II. *Newspapers* 報社

- Central Daily News　　　　　　中央日報
- China Times　　　　　　　　　中國時報
- China Times Express　　　　　　中時晚報
- Commercial Times　　　　　　　工商時報
- Economic Daily News　　　　　　經濟日報
- Finance & Economic Times　　　財經時報
- Fortune Daily News　　　　　　財星日報
- Gwoyeu Ryhbaw　　　　　　　　國語日報
- Min Sheng Pao　　　　　　　　民生報
- Taiwan Shin Sheng Daily News　台灣新生報
- United Daily News　　　　　　聯合報
- United Evening News　　　　　聯合晚報
- Wealth News　　　　　　　　　財訊快報

- Youth Daily News ┊ 青年日報
- The China News ┊ 英文中國日報
- The China Post ┊ 英文中國郵報
- The Great News ┊ 大成報
- The Independence Evening Post ┊ 自立晚報

Ⅲ. *Radio Stations* 廣播電台

- Broadcasting Corporation of China ┊ 中國廣播公司
- Central Broadcasting System of the R.O.C. ┊ 中央廣播電台
- Cheng Sheng Broadcasting Corp. Ltd. ┊ 正聲廣播公司
- China Broadcasting Co. ┊ 中華廣播公司
- China Youth Broadcasting Station ┊ 幼獅廣播電台
- The Voice of Han Broadcasting Network ┊ 漢聲廣播電台
- Fu Hsing Broadcasting Station ┊ 復興廣播電台
- International Community Radio Taipei (*ICRT*) ┊ 台北國際社區廣播電台
- Kaohsiung Broadcasting Station ┊ 高雄廣播電台
- Public Radio System ┊ 警察廣播電台
- Taipei Broadcasting Station ┊ 台北廣播電台
- Taiwan Broadcasting Co., Ltd. ┊ 臺灣廣播公司
- Educational Broadcasting System ┊ 教育廣播電台

Ⅳ. *Television Stations* 電視公司

- Chinese Public Television, the Broadcasting Development Fund ┊ 廣播電視事業發展基金公共電視組
- Television Broadcasting Station ┊ TVBS

- China Television Co. Ltd. (*CTV*)　　中國電視公司
- Chinese Television System (*CTS*)　　中華電視台
- Taiwan Television Enterprise, Ltd　　臺灣電視公司
  (*TTV*)

V. *Magazines* 雜誌

- Asia Week　　　　　　　　　　　亞洲週刊
- Blanca　　　　　　　　　　　　博覽家雜誌
- Car Magazine　　　　　　　　　汽車購買指南
- China Times Weekly　　　　　　時報週刊
- Commonwealth-Taiwan's Leading　天下雜誌
  Magazine
- Diana　　　　　　　　　　　　黛
- Evergreen　　　　　　　　　　常春
- Global Views Monthly　　　　　遠見
- Hsiung Shih Art Monthly　　　　雄獅美術月刊
- Japan Digest　　　　　　　　　日本文摘
- Modern Home　　　　　　　　　摩登家庭
- Money　　　　　　　　　　　　錢
- Music & Audiophile　　　　　　音樂與音響
- Newsweek　　　　　　　　　　美國新聞週刊
- Newton　　　　　　　　　　　牛頓雜誌
- Reader's Digest　　　　　　　　讀者文摘
- The Journalist　　　　　　　　新新聞週刊
- Unitas　　　　　　　　　　　聯合文學
- Wealth Magazine　　　　　　　財訊
- World Geographic Magazine　　　世界地理雜誌
- World Screen　　　　　　　　　世界電影
- Time　　　　　　　　　　　　時代雜誌

中華民國政府機構
The Organizations of the Republic of China

I. *The Central Government* 中央政府

☆ Office of the President　總統府

☆ National Security Council 國家安全會議

• National Security Bureau　國家安全局

☆ National Assembly 國民大會

☆ National Unification Council　國家統一委員會

☆ Executive Yuan　行政院

☆ Legislative Yuan　立法院

☆ Judicial Yuan　司法院

• Supreme Court　最高法院

• Administrative Court　行政法院

• Committee on the Discipline of Public Functionaries
公務員懲戒委員會

☆ Examination Yuan　考試院

• Ministry of Examination　考選部

• Ministry of Personnel　銓敘部

☆ Control Yuan 監察院

• Ministry of Auditing　審計部

II. *The Cabinet* 行政院所屬各部會

☆ Ministry of the Interior（*MOI*）內政部

• National Police Administration　警政署

• Criminal Investigation Bureau　刑事警察局

- Bureau of Entry & Exit 入出境管理局
☆ Ministry of Foreign Affairs (*MOFA*) 外交部
☆ Ministry of National Defense (*MND*) 國防部
☆ Ministry of Finance (*MOF*) 財政部
- Directorate General of Customs 關稅總局
☆ Ministry of Education (*MOE*) 教育部
☆ Ministry of Justice (*MOJ*) 法務部
☆ Ministry of Economic Affairs (*MOEA*) 經濟部
- Bureau of Commodity Inspection & Quarantine 商品檢驗局
☆ Ministry of Transportation and Communications (*MOTC*) 交通部
- Directorate General of Posts 郵政總局
- Civil Aeronautics Administration 民航局
- Directorate General of Telecommunications 電信總局
- Taiwan Area National Freeway Bureau 台灣區國道高速公路局
- Tourism Bureau 觀光局
- Government Information Office 新聞局
- Central Personnel Administration 人事行政局
☆ Council for Economic Planning and Development 經濟建設委員會
☆ Council for Cultural Planning and Development 文化建設委員會
☆ Mainland Affairs Council 大陸事務委員會
- Environmental Protection Administration 環保署

II. *Provincial government organizations* 省級機構

☆ Taiwan Provincial Government 台灣省政府
- Chung Hsin New Village 中興新村
☆ Taiwan Provincial Council 省議會

- Department of Civil Affairs 民政廳
- Department of Finance 財政廳
- Taiwan Tobacco & Wine Monopoly Bureau 煙酒公賣局
- Department of Reconstruction 建設廳
- Water Conservancy Bureau 水利局
- Department of Education 教育廳
- Department of Agriculture & Forestry 農林廳
- Forestry Bureau 林務局
- Fishery Bureau 漁業局
- Department of Communications 交通處
- Taiwan Railway Administration 鐵路局
- Taiwan Highway Bureau 公路局
- Highway Supervision Office 監理處
- Taiwan Bus Transportation Co. 臺灣汽車客運公司
- Harbors Bureau 港務局
- Department of Social Affairs 社會處
- Bureau of Labor Insurance 勞工保險局
- Taiwan Quarantine Station 檢疫所
- Food Bureau 糧食局
- The Taiwan Provincial Archives 臺灣省文獻委員會
- County Government 縣政府

Ⅳ. *Municipal government organizations* 地方機構

☆ The Municipal Government of Taipei 台北市政府
☆ Taipei City Council 市議會
- Tax Collection Office 稅捐稽徵處
- Bureau of Public Works 工務局
- Environmental Sanitation Department 環境清潔處

- Citizen's Employment Guidance Office　國民就業輔導處
- District Administration Office　區公所
- Town Administration Office　鎮公所
- Hsiang Administration Office　鄉公所
- Taipei District Prosecutor's Office　台北地檢處

V. *Titles of Government Officials*　政府官員稱謂

- ☆ President of the ROC　中華民國總統
- ☆ Vice President　副總統
- ☆ Premier　行政院長
- ☆ Vice Premier　行政院副院長
- ☆ Presidents of Five Yuans　五院院長
- ☆ Vice President　副院長
- Minister　部長
- Vice Minister　次長
- Political Vice-Minister　政務次長
- Administrative Vice-Minister　常務次長
- Chairman of Commission or Committee　委員會委員長
- Director　廳長、司長、局長、主任
- Commissioner　廠長、專員
- Counselor　參事
- Mayor　市長
- Magistrate　縣長
- Township/District/Village Chief　鎮長/區長/鄉長
- Section Chief　組長、科長

美國政府機構
The Organizations of the United States

Ⅰ. *The U.S. Government* 美國政府

☆ The Federal Government 聯邦政府

☆ The White House 白宮

- Chief of the White House Staff 白宮主任
- Special Assistant to the President for National Security Affairs 負責國家安全事務的總統特別助理
- Adviser on Domestic and Foreign Matters 國內外事務顧問
- Council of Economic Advisers 經濟顧問委員會
- National Security Council 國家安全委員會
- Central Intelligence Agency (*CIA*) 中央情報局

Ⅱ. *The Cabinet* 內閣

☆ Department of State 國務院

- Secretary of State 國務卿
- Deputy Secretary of State 副國務卿

☆ Department of Defense 國防部

- The Pentagon 五角大廈
- Secretary of Defense 國防部長

☆ Department of Interior 內政部

☆ Department of Treasury 財政部

☆ Department of Labor 勞工部

☆ Department of Commerce　商業部

☆ Department of Agriculture　農業部

☆ Department of Justice　司法部

· Attorney General　司法部長

☆ Post Office Department　郵務部

· Postmaster General　郵政總監

☆ Department of Health, Education, and Welfare
　衛生、教育及福利部

☆ Department of Housing and Urban Development
　住屋及城市發展部

☆ Department of Transportation　運輸部

☆ Department of Energy　能源部

III. *The Congress* 國會

☆ The Capitol Hill　國會議場

· Congressman / Lawmaker / Solon　國會議員

☆ The Senate　參議院

· Senator　參議員

☆ The House of Representatives / The House　衆議院

· Representative　衆議員

☆ National Legislature　聯邦國會

☆ Republican Party / GOP (*Grand Old Party*)
　共和黨《 Elephant 》

☆ Democratic Party　共和黨《 Donkey 》

· Majority Leader　多數黨領袖

· Minority Leader　少數黨領袖

IV. *Local Government* 地方政府

- ☆ State Legislature 州議會
- ☆ State Government 州政府
- · Governor 州長
- ☆ Washington, D.C. (*District of Columbia*) 哥倫比亞特區
- · Commissioner 專員（通稱 *Mayor* 市長）
- ☆ County 郡
- · Commission Chairman 郡長
- ☆ City 市
- · Mayor 市長

V. *The Court* 法院

- ☆ The Supreme Court of the United States 美國最高法院
- · Chief Justice 聯邦最高法院院長
- · Associate Justice 最高法院推事
- ☆ The Supreme Court of the State 州最高法院
- · Chief Judge 院長
- · Associate Judge 推事
- ☆ United States Court of Appeals 美國上訴院
- ☆ United States District Court 美國地方法院

美國五十州及首府

The Fifty States and Capitals of the United States

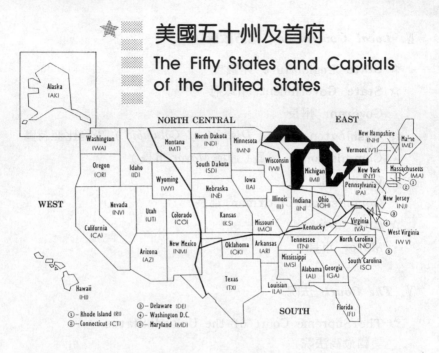

州　　　　　　　　　名	縮寫	首　　　府
Alabama 〔͵ælə'bæmə〕 阿拉巴馬	AL	Montgomery 蒙哥馬利
Alaska 〔ə'læskə〕 阿拉斯加	AK	Juneau 朱諾
Arizona 〔͵ærə'zonə〕 亞利桑那	AZ	Phoenix 鳳凰城
Arkansas 〔'ɑrkən͵sɔ〕 阿肯色	AR	Little Rock 小巖
California 〔͵kælə'fɔrnɪə〕 加利福尼亞	CA	Sacramento 薩克拉曼多
Colorado 〔͵kɑlə'rɑdo〕 科羅拉多	CO	Denver 丹佛
Connecticut 〔kə'nɛtɪkət〕 康乃狄克	CT	Hartford 哈特福特
Delaware 〔'dɛlə͵wɛr〕 德拉威	DE	Dover 多佛
Florida 〔'flɔrədə〕 佛羅里達	FL	Tallahassee 塔拉哈西
Georgia 〔'dʒɔrdʒə〕 喬治亞	GA	Atlanta 亞特蘭大
Hawaii 〔hə'waɪ·i〕 夏威夷	HI	Honolulu 檀香山
Idaho 〔'aɪdɪ͵ho〕 愛達荷	ID	Boise 波易士

州　　　　　　　　　　名	縮寫	首　　　　　　府
Illinois〔͵ɪləˋnɔɪz〕伊利諾	I L	Springfield 春田
Indiana〔͵ɪndɪˋænə〕印地安納	I N	Indianapolis 印第安納波里
Iowa〔ˋaɪəwə〕愛荷華	I A	Des Moines 第蒙
Kansas〔ˋkænzəs〕堪薩斯	K S	Topeka 托皮卡
Kentucky〔kənˋtʌkɪ〕肯塔基	K Y	Frankfort 法蘭克福
Louisiana〔͵luɪzɪˋænə〕路易斯安那	L A	Baton Rouge 巴頓魯治
Maine〔men〕緬因	M E	Augusta 奧古斯坦
Maryland〔ˋmɛrɪlənd〕馬里蘭	M D	Annapolis 亞那波里
Massachusetts〔͵mæsəˋtʃusɪts〕麻薩諸塞	M A	Boston 波士頓
Michigan〔ˋmɪʃəgən〕密西根	M I	Lansing 蘭辛
Minnesota〔͵mɪnɪˋsotə〕明尼蘇達	M N	Saint Paul 聖保羅
Mississippi〔͵mɪsəˋsɪpɪ〕密西西比	M S	Jackson 傑克生
Missouri〔məˋzʊrɪ〕米蘇里	M O	Jefferson City 傑佛遜市
Montana〔mɑnˋtænə〕蒙大拿	M T	Helena 赫勒拿
Nebraska〔nəˋbræskə〕內布拉斯加	N B	Lincoln 林肯市
Nevada〔nəˋvædə〕內華達	N V	Carson City 喀生市
New Hampshire〔njuˋhæmpʃɪr〕新罕布夏	N H	Concord 康科特
New Jersey〔njuˋdʒɝzɪ〕新澤西	N J	Trenton 特稜頓
New Mexico〔njuˋmɛksɪ͵ko〕新墨西哥	N M	Santa Fe 聖大非
New York〔njuˋjɔrk〕紐約	N Y	Albany 奧爾班尼

州　　　　　　　　名	縮寫	首　　　府
North Carolina〔nɔrθ,kærəˈlaɪnə〕北卡羅來納	NC	Raleigh 洛利
North Dakota〔nɔrθ,dəˈkotə〕北達科塔	ND	Bismarck 俾斯麥市
Ohio〔oˈhaɪo〕俄亥俄	OH	Columbus 哥倫布市
Oklahoma〔,okləˈhomə〕奧克拉荷馬	OK	Oklahoma City 奧克拉荷馬市
Oregon〔ˈɑrɪ,ɡan〕俄勒岡	OR	Salem〔ˈseləm〕賽倫
Pennsylvania〔,pɛnsḷˈvenjə〕賓夕凡尼亞	PA	Harrisburg 哈立斯堡
Rhode Island〔rodˈaɪlənd〕羅德島	RI	Providence 普洛維頓斯
South Carolina〔saʊθ,kærəˈlaɪnə〕南卡羅來納	SC	Columbia 哥倫比亞市
South Dakota〔saʊθ,dəˈkotə〕南達科塔	SD	Pierre 皮耳
Tennessee〔ˈtɛnə,si〕田納西	TN	Nashville 那士維
Texas〔ˈtɛksəs〕德克薩斯	TX	Austin 奧斯丁
Utah〔ˈjuta〕猶他	UT	Salt Lake City 鹽湖城
Vermont〔vəˈmant〕佛蒙特	VT	Montpelier 蒙皮立
Virginia〔vəˈdʒmjə〕維吉亞	VA	Richmond 利其蒙
Washington〔ˈwaʃɪŋtən〕華盛頓	WA	Olympia 奧林匹克
West Virginia〔wɛst,vəˈdʒɪnjə〕西維吉尼亞	WV	Charleston 查理斯頓
Wisconsin〔wɪsˈkɑnsṇ〕威斯康辛	WI	Madison 麥廸孫市
Wyoming〔ˈwaɪəmɪŋ〕懷俄明	WY	Cheyenne 夏安市

世界各國及首都
The Countries and Capitals of the World

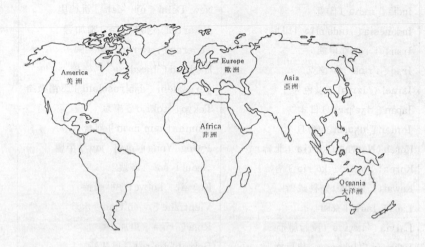

✦ASIA 亞洲✦	
國　　　　　　　名	首　　　　　　　都
Afghanistan〔æfˈɡænə͵stæn〕阿富汗	Kabul〔ˈkɑbʊl〕喀布爾
Armenia〔ɑrˈminɪə〕亞美尼亞	Erivan〔͵jɪrjɪˈvɑn〕城里溫
Azerbaijan〔͵æzə͵baɪˈdʒɑn〕亞塞拜然	Baku〔bɑˈku〕巴庫
Bahrain〔bəˈraɪn〕巴林	Manama〔məˈnæmə〕麥納瑪
Bangladesh〔ˈbæŋɡlə͵dɛʃ〕孟加拉	Dacca〔ˈdækə〕達卡
Belorussia〔bjɪlʌˈrussjrjə〕白俄羅斯	Minsk〔mɪnsk〕明斯克
Bhutan〔bʊˈtɑn〕不丹	Thimbu〔ˈθɪmbu〕辛布
Brunei〔brʊˈnaɪ〕汶萊	Bandar Seri Begawan〔͵bʌndə ͵sɛrɪ bəˈɡɑwən〕斯里巴加萬港
Burma〔ˈbɝmə〕緬甸	Rangoon〔ˈræŋɡun〕仰光
Cyprus〔ˈsaɪprəs〕塞普勒斯	Nicosia〔͵nɪkoˈsiə〕尼科西亞

國　　　　名	首　　　　都
Cambodia〔kæmˈboɪdɪə〕高棉	Phnom Penh〔pəˈnɔm ˈpɛn〕金邊
Estonia〔ɛsˈtonɪə〕愛沙尼亞	Tallinn〔ˈtælɪn〕塔林
Georgia〔ˈdʒɔrdʒjə〕喬治亞	Tiflis〔ˈtɪflɪs〕提弗利司
India〔ˈɪndɪə〕印度	New Delhi〔nju ˈdɛlɪ〕新德里
Indonesia〔ˌɪndoˈniʃə〕印尼	Jakarta〔dʒəˈkartə〕雅加達
Iran〔iˈran〕伊朗	Teheran〔ˌtɪəˈran〕德黑蘭
Iraq〔ɪˈræk〕伊拉克	Baghdad〔ˈbægdæd〕巴格達
Israel〔ˈɪzrɪəl〕以色列	Jerusalem〔dʒəˈrusələm〕耶路撒冷
Japan〔dʒəˈpæn〕日本	Tokyo〔ˈtokɪˌo〕東京
Jordan〔ˈdʒɔrdṇ〕約旦	Amman〔æmˈmæn〕阿曼
Korea(North)〔koˈriə〕北韓	Pyong Yang〔ˈpjʌŋ ˈjɑn〕平壤
Korea(South)〔koˈriə〕南韓	Seoul〔sol〕漢城
Kuwait〔kʊˈwet〕科威特	Kuwait〔kʊˈwet〕科威特
Laos〔laʊz〕寮國	Vientiane〔ˌvjɛnˈtjan〕永珍
Latvia〔ˈlætvɪə〕拉脫維亞	Riga〔ˈrɪgə〕里加
Lebanon〔ˈlɛbənən〕黎巴嫩	Beirut〔beˈrut〕貝魯特
Lithuania〔ˌlɪθjʊˈenɪə〕立陶宛	Vilnius〔ˈvɪlnə〕維尼斯
Malaysia〔məˈleʒə〕馬來西亞	Kuala Lumpur〔ˈkwalə ˈlʊmpʊr〕吉隆坡
Maldive Islands〔ˈmældaɪv ˈaɪləndz〕馬爾地夫	Male〔mel〕馬爾
Mongolia〔mɑŋˈgoljə〕蒙古	Kulun〔ˈkuˈlun〕庫倫
Nepal〔nɪˈpɔl〕尼泊爾	Katmandu〔ˌkatmanˈdu〕加德滿都
Oman〔oˈmæn〕阿曼	Muscat〔ˈmʌskət〕馬斯科特
Pakistan〔ˌpakɪˈstan〕巴基斯坦	Islamabad〔ɪsˈlaməbad〕伊斯蘭馬巴德
Philippines〔ˈfɪləˌpinz〕菲律賓	Manila〔məˈnɪlə〕馬尼拉
Qatar〔ˈkatar〕卡達	Doha〔ˈdohə〕杜哈
Russia〔ˈrʌʃə〕俄羅斯	Moscow〔ˈmasko〕莫斯科

國　　　　名	首　　　　都
Saudi Arabia〔sɑˊudɪ əˊrebɪə〕沙烏地阿拉伯	Riyadh〔rɪˊjɑd〕利雅得
Singapore〔ˊsɪŋgəˏpor〕新加坡	Singapore〔ˊsɪŋgəˏpor〕新加坡
Southern Yemen〔ˊsʌðən ˊjɛmən〕南葉門	Aden〔ˊedn̩〕亞丁
Sri Lanka〔ˏsrɪˊlæŋkə〕斯里蘭卡	Colombo〔kəˊlʌmbo〕可倫坡
Syria〔ˊsɪrɪə〕敘利亞	Damascus〔dəˊmæskəs〕大馬士革
Thailand〔ˊtaɪlənd〕泰國	Bangkok〔ˊbæŋkɑk〕曼谷
The Republic of China〔ðə rɪˊpʌblɪk əv ˊtʃaɪnə〕中華民國	Taipei〔ˊtaɪˏpe〕台北
Turkey〔ˊtɝkɪ〕土耳其	Ankara〔ˊɑŋkərə〕安卡拉
Ukraine〔ˊjukren〕烏克蘭	Kiev〔ˊkiˏɛf〕基輔
United Arab Emirates〔juˊnaɪtɪd ˊærəb əˊmɪrɪts〕阿拉伯聯合大公國	Abu Dhabi〔ˏɑbu ˊdæbɪ〕阿布達比
Vietnam〔ˏvietˊnɑm〕越南	Hanoi〔hɑˊnɔɪ〕河內
Yemen〔ˊjɛmən〕葉門	Sanaa〔ˊsænˏɑ〕沙那

✦ AFRICA 非洲 ✦	
國　　　　名	首　　　　都
Algeria〔ælˊdʒɪrɪə〕阿爾及利亞	Algiers〔ælˊdʒɪrz〕阿爾及耳
Angola〔æŋˊgolə〕安哥拉	Luanda〔luˊændə〕盧安達
Dahomey〔dəˊhomɪ〕達荷美	Porto-Novo〔ˏportəˊnovo〕新港
Botswana〔bɑtsˊwɑnɑ〕波札那	Gaborone〔ˊgɑbəˊron〕嘉柏隆
Burundi〔bəˊrʌndɪ〕蒲隆地	Bujumbura〔ˏbudʒəmˊburə〕布松布拉
Cameroon〔ˏkæməˊrun〕喀麥隆	Yaounde〔jɑʊnˊde〕雅溫得
Cape Verde〔ˊkep ˏvɝd〕維德角	Praia〔ˊpraɪə〕培賴亞
Central African Rep.〔ˊsɛntrəl ˊæfrɪkən rɪˊpʌblɪk〕中非	Bangui〔bɑŋˊgi〕班基
Chad〔tʃɑd〕查德	Ndjamena〔ɛnˊdʒɑmənə〕恩將納
Comoro〔ˊkɑməro〕科摩羅	Moroni〔moˊrɑnɪ〕莫拉尼

國　　　　名	首　　　　都
Congo〔ˊkɑŋgo〕剛果	Brazzaville〔ˊbræzəvɪl〕布拉扎維
Djibouti〔dʒəˊbutɪ〕吉布地共和國	Djibouti〔dʒəˊbutɪ〕吉布地
Egypt〔ˊidʒɪpt〕埃及	Cairo〔ˊkaɪro〕開羅
Ethiopia〔ˌiθɪˊopɪə〕衣索匹亞	Addis Ababa〔ˊædɪs ˊæbəbə〕阿廸斯阿貝巴
Gabon〔ˌgɑˊbõ〕加彭	Libreville〔ˊlɪbrəˌvɪl〕自由市
Gambia〔ˊgæmbɪə〕甘比亞	Banjul〔ˊbɑnˌdʒul〕班竹
Ghana〔ˊgɑnə〕迦納	Accra〔ˊækrə〕阿克拉
Guinea〔ˊgɪnɪ〕幾內亞	Conakry〔kɑnˊkri〕康那克立
Guinea-Bissau〔ˊgɪnɪ bɪˊsɑu〕幾內亞－比索	Bissau〔bɪsˊɑu〕比索
Ivory Coast〔ˊaɪvərɪ ˌkost〕象牙海岸	Abidjan〔ˊæbɪˌdʒɑn〕阿必尚
Kenya〔ˊkɛnjə〕肯亞	Nairobi〔naɪˊrobɪ〕奈洛比
Lesotho〔ləˊsoto〕賴索托	Maseru〔ˊmæzəˌru〕馬塞魯
Liberia〔laɪˊbɪrɪə〕賴比瑞亞	Monrovia〔mənˊrovɪə〕門羅維亞
Libya〔ˊlɪbɪə〕利比亞	Tripoli〔ˊtrɪpəlɪ〕的黎波里
Madagascar〔ˌmædəˊgæskɚ〕馬達加斯加	Tananarive〔ˌtɑˌnɑˌnɑˊriv〕塔那那利夫
Malawi〔mɑˊlawi〕馬拉威	Lilongwe〔lɪˊlɔŋwe〕里郎威
Mali〔ˊmɑlɪ〕馬利	Bamako〔ˌbɑməˊko〕巴馬科
Mauritania〔ˌmɔrɪˊtenɪə〕茅利塔尼亞	Nouakchott〔nwakˊʃɑt〕那瓦克夏特
Mauritius〔mɔˊrɪʃɪəs〕模里西斯	Port Louis〔ˊpɔrt ˌluɪs〕路易斯港
Morocco〔məˊrako〕摩洛哥	Rabat〔rəˊbat〕拉巴特
Mozambique〔ˌmozəmˊbik〕莫三比克	Maputo〔mɑˊputo〕馬布多
Niger〔ˊnaɪdʒɚ〕尼日	Niamey〔njɑˊme〕尼亞美
Nigeria〔naɪˊdʒɪrɪə〕奈及利亞	Lagos〔ˊlegəs〕拉哥斯
Rwanda〔ruˊandə〕盧安達	Kigali〔ˊkɪgəlɪ〕吉加利
São Tomé〔ˊsãuntuˊmɛ〕聖圖美島	São Tomé〔ˊsãuntuˊmɛ〕聖圖美
Senegal〔ˌsɛnɪˊgɔl〕塞內加爾	Dakar〔dɑˊkɑr〕達喀爾

國　　名	首　　都
Seychelles〔seˈʃɛlz〕塞昔耳	Victoria〔vɪkˈtorɪə〕維多利亞
Sierra Leone〔sɪˈɛrəlɪˈoni〕獅子山	Freetown〔ˈfriˌtaʊn〕自由城
Somalia〔səˈmɑlɪə〕索馬利亞	Mogadishu〔ˌmɑgəˈdɪʃɪo〕摩加底休
South Africa〔saʊθ ˈæfrɪkə〕南非	Pretoria〔prɪˈtorɪə〕普勒多利亞
Sudan〔suˈdæn〕蘇丹	Khartoum〔kɑrˈtum〕喀土木
Swaziland〔ˈswɑzɪˌlænd〕史瓦濟蘭	Mbabane〔ˌɛmbəˈban〕墨巴本
Tanzania〔ˌtænzəˈniə〕坦尚尼亞	Dar es Salaam〔ˌdɑrˌɛs səˈlɑm〕達萊撒蘭
Togo〔ˈtogo〕多哥	Lome〔ˌlɔˈme〕勞梅
Transkei〔trænsˈkaɪ〕川斯凱	Umtata〔ʊmˈtɑtə〕翁塔達
Tunisia〔tjuˈnɪʃɪə〕突尼西亞	Tunis〔ˈtjunɪs〕突尼斯
Uganda〔juˈgændə〕烏干達	Kampala〔kɑmˈpɑlɑ〕康帕拉
Venda〔ˈvɛndɑ〕溫達	Thohoyandou〔toˌhɔɪænˈdu〕托赫揚度
Zaire〔zəˈirə〕薩伊	Kinshasa〔kɪnˈʃɑsə〕金夏沙
Zambia〔ˈzæmˈbɪə〕尚比亞	Lusaka〔luˈsɑkə〕路沙卡

✦ EUROPE 歐洲 ✦

國　　名	首　　都
Albania〔ælˈbenɪə〕阿爾巴尼亞	Tirane〔tɪˈrɑnɑ〕地拉那
Andorra〔ænˈdɔrə〕安道爾	Andorra〔ænˈdɔrə〕安道爾
Austria〔ˈɔstrɪə〕奧地利	Vienna〔vɪˈɛnə〕維也那
Belgium〔ˈbɛldʒɪəm〕比利時	Brussels〔ˈbrʌslz〕布魯塞爾
Bulgaria〔bʌlˈgɛrɪə〕保加利亞	Sofia〔ˈsofɪə〕蘇非亞
Czech Republic〔ˌtʃɛk rɪˈpʌblɪk〕捷克共和國	Prague〔prɑg〕布拉格
Denmark〔ˈdɛnmɑrk〕丹麥	Copenhagen〔ˌkopənˈhegən〕哥本哈根
Finland〔ˈfɪnlənd〕芬蘭	Helsinki〔ˈhɛlsɪŋkɪ〕赫爾辛基
France〔fræns〕法國	Paris〔ˈpærɪs〕巴黎

國 名	首 都
Germany〔ˈdʒɝˈmənɪ〕德國	Berlin〔bɝˈlɪn〕柏林
Great Britain〔ˈbrɪtən〕英國	London〔ˈlʌndən〕倫敦
Greece〔gris〕希臘	Athens〔ˈæθənz〕雅典
Hungary〔ˈhʌŋgərɪ〕匈牙利	Budapest〔ˌbjudəˈpɛst〕布達佩斯
Iceland〔ˈaɪslənd〕冰島	Reykjavik〔ˈrekjɑˌvik〕雷克雅未克
Ireland〔ˈaɪrlənd〕愛爾蘭	Dublin〔ˈdʌblɪn〕都柏林
Italy〔ˈɪtḷɪ〕義大利	Rome〔rom〕羅馬
Liechtenstein〔ˈlɪktənˌstaɪn〕 列支敦士敦	Vaduz〔vɑˈduts〕瓦都茲
Luxembourg〔ˈlʌksəmˌbɝg〕盧森堡	Luxembourg〔ˈlʌksəmˌbɝg〕盧森堡
Malta〔ˈmɔltə〕馬爾他	Valletta〔vəˈlɛtə〕瓦勒塔
Monaco〔ˈmɑnəˌko〕摩納哥	Monte Carlo〔ˌmɑntɪˈkɑrlo〕蒙地卡羅
Netherlands〔ˈnɛðəlǝndz〕荷蘭	Amsterdam〔ˈæmstəˌdæm〕 阿姆斯特丹
Norway〔ˈnɔrwe〕挪威	Oslo〔ˈɑzlo〕奧斯陸
Poland〔ˈpolənd〕波蘭	Warsaw〔ˈwɔrsɔ〕華沙
Portugal〔ˈportʃəgḷ〕葡萄牙	Lisbon〔ˈlɪzbən〕里斯本
Romania〔roˈmenjə〕羅馬尼亞	Bucharest〔ˌbukəˈrɛst〕布加勒斯特
San Marino〔ˌsæn məˈrino〕 聖馬利諾	San Marino〔ˌsæn məˈrino〕 聖馬利諾
Slovakia〔sloˈvækɪə〕斯洛伐克	Bratislava〔ˌbrætəˈslɑvə〕 伯拉第斯拉克
Spain〔spen〕西班牙	Madrid〔məˈdrɪd〕馬德里
Sweden〔ˈswidṇ〕瑞典	Stockholm〔ˈstɑkˌhom〕斯德哥爾摩
Switzerland〔ˈswɪtsələnd〕瑞士	Berne〔bɝn〕伯恩
Vatican City〔ˈvætɪkən ˈsɪtɪ〕梵諦岡	Vatican City〔ˈvætɪkən ˈsɪtɪ〕梵諦岡

✦ OCEANIA 大洋洲 ✦

國 名	首 都
Australia〔ɔˈstreljə〕澳大利亞	Canberra〔ˈkænbərə〕坎培拉

國　　　　名	首　　　　都
Fiji〔ˈfidʒi〕斐濟	Suva〔ˈsuvə〕蘇瓦
Kiribati〔ˈkɪrəˌbæs〕基里巴斯	Tarawa〔təˈrɑwə〕塔拉瓦
New Zealand〔njuˈzilənd〕紐西蘭	Wellington〔ˈwɛlɪŋtən〕威靈頓
Papua New Guinea〔ˈpæpjuə njuˈgɪnɪ〕巴布新幾內亞	Port Moresby〔pɔrtˈmorzbɪ〕摩爾斯貝港
Samoa〔səˈmoə〕薩摩亞	Apia〔ɑˈpiɑ〕阿比亞
Solomon〔ˈsɑləmən〕所羅門	Honiara〔ˌhoniˈɑrə〕荷尼阿拉
Tonga〔ˈtɑŋgə〕東加	Nukualofa〔ˌnukəwəˈlɔfə〕努瓜婁發
Tuvalu〔tuˈvalu〕吐瓦魯	Funafuti〔ˌfunəˈfuti〕富那富提

✦ AMERICA 美洲 ✦

國　　　　名	首　　　　都
Argentina〔ˌɑrdʒənˈtinə〕阿根廷	Buenos Aires〔ˈbonəs ˈɛriz〕布宜若
Bahamas〔bəˈhɑməz〕巴哈馬	Nassau〔ˈnæsɔ〕拿梭
Barbados〔ˈbɑrbəˌdoz〕巴貝多	Bridgetown〔ˈbrɪdʒˌtɑun〕橋城
Bolivia〔bəˈlɪvɪə〕玻利維亞	La Pas〔la ˈpas〕拉巴斯
Brazil〔brəˈzɪl〕巴西	Brasilia〔brəˈziljə〕巴西利亞
Canada〔ˈkænədə〕加拿大	Ottawa〔ˈɑtəwə〕渥太華
Chile〔ˈtʃɪlɪ〕智利	Santiago〔ˌsæntiˈɑgo〕聖地牙哥
Colombia〔kəˈlʌmbɪə〕哥倫比亞	Bogota〔ˌbogəˈtɑ〕波哥大
Costa Rica〔ˈkɑstəˈrikə〕哥斯大黎加	San Jose〔ˌsanhoˈsɛ〕聖荷西
Cuba〔ˈkjubə〕古巴	Havana〔həˈvænə〕哈瓦那
Dominica〔dəˈmɪnɪkə〕多明尼加	Roseau〔roˈzo〕羅梭
Dominican Rep.〔dəˈmɪnɪkən rɪˈpʌblɪk〕多明尼加共和國	Santo Domingo〔ˈsæntodəˈmɪŋgo〕聖多明哥
Ecuador〔ˈɛkwəˌdɔr〕厄瓜多爾	Quito〔ˈkito〕基多
El Salvador〔ɛl ˈsælvəˌdɔr〕薩爾瓦多	San Salvador〔sæn ˈsælvəˌdɔr〕聖薩爾瓦多

國　　　　　名	首　　　　　都
Grenada〔grɪˈnedə〕格瑞內達	St. Georges〔sent ˈdʒɔrdʒɪz〕聖喬治
Guatemala〔ˌgwɑtəˈmɑlə〕瓜地馬拉	Guatemala City〔ˌgwɑtəˈmɑlə ˈsɪtɪ〕瓜地馬拉市
Guyana〔gaɪˈænə〕蓋亞那	Georgetown〔ˈdʒɔrdʒɪˌtaʊn〕喬治城
Haiti〔ˈhetɪ〕海地	Port-Au-Prince〔ˌportoˈprɪns〕太子港
Honduras〔hɑnˈdʊrəs〕宏都拉斯	Tegucigalpa〔təˌgusɪˈgælpə〕特古西加帕
Jamaica〔dʒəˈmekə〕牙買加	Kingston〔ˈkɪŋstən〕京斯敦
Mexico〔ˈmɛksɪˌko〕墨西哥	Mexico City〔ˈmɛksɪˌko ˈsɪtɪ〕墨西哥城
Nicaragua〔ˌnɪkəˈrɑgwə〕尼加拉瓜	Managua〔məˈnɑgwə〕馬拿瓜
Panama〔ˈpænəˌmɑ〕巴拿馬	Panama City〔ˈpænəˌmɑ ˈsɪtɪ〕巴拿巴城
Paraguay〔ˈpærəˌgwe〕巴拉圭	Asuncion〔ˌɑsunˈsjon〕亞松森
Peru〔pəˈru〕秘魯	Lima〔ˈlimə〕利馬
St. Lucia〔sent ˈluʃɪə〕聖露西亞	Castries〔ˈkæsˌtriz〕卡斯翠
St. Vincent〔sent ˈvɪnsn̩t〕聖文生	Kingstown〔ˈkɪŋsˌtaʊn〕王城
Surinam〔ˌsʊrɪˈnɑm〕蘇利南	Paramaribo〔ˌpærəˈmærəˌbo〕巴拉馬利波
The United States〔ðə jʊˈnaɪtɪd stets〕美國	Washington D.C.〔ˈwaʃɪntən〕華盛頓特區
Trinidad-Tobago〔ˈtrɪnəˌdæd təˈbego〕千里達－托貝哥	Port-Spain〔ˈportˌspen〕西班牙港
Uruguay〔ˈjʊrəˌgwe〕烏拉圭	Montevideo〔ˌmɑntəvɪˈdeo〕孟特維得亞
Venezuela〔ˌvɛnəˈzwilə〕委內瑞拉	Caracas〔kaˈrakas〕加拉卡斯

解　答

《英文報紙閱讀訣竅》

p.5 … 1. ROC is not likely to be targeted
　　　 2. The chief is absent from meeting on defense
　　　 3. Ozone layer is thinner over Europe
　　　 4. Europe team is to face the heat
　　　 5. A former university teacher is arrested

p.8 … *B*　　　p.12 … 1. *B*　　2. *C*　　3. *A*

《社會文化》

p.15 … 1. *C*　　2. *A*　　3. *A*　　　　　p.17 … 1. *B*　　2. *A*
p.19 … *C*　　　　　　　　　　　　　　　　p.22 … 1. *D*　　2. *B*　　3. *B*　　4. *D*
p.27 … 1. *C*　　2. *A*　　3. *B*　　　　　p.30 … 1. *C*　　2. *B*　　3. *D*　　4. *B*
p.33 … 1. *C*　　2. *C*　　3. *C*　　　　　p.35 … *C*
p.38 … 1. *A*　　2. *C*　　3. *D*　　　　　p.43 … 1. *D*　　2. *B*　　3. *C*　　4. *C*
p.46 … 1. *D*　　2. *A*　　3. *B*　　　　　p.49 … 1. *C*　　2. *B*　　3. *C*
p.51 … *B*　　　　　　　　　　　　　　　　p.54 … 1. *C*　　2. *C*　　3. *D*
p.57 … 1. *D*　　2. *A*　　3. *B*

《政治軍事》

p.61 … 1. *B*　　2. *D*　　3. *A*　　　　　p.64 … 1. *C*　　2. *A*　　3. *C*　　4. *B*
p.67 … 1. *C*　　2. *B*　　　　　　　　　　p.72 … 1. *C*　　2. *A*　　3. *B*　　4. *A*
p.75 … 1. *D*　　2. *A*　　3. *B*　　　　　p.79 … 1. *C*　　2. *B*　　3. *B*
p.84 … 1. *D*　　2. *C*　　3. *A*　　4. *B*　p.87 … 1. *C*　　2. *A*　　3. *C*
p.90 … 1. *D*　　2. *A*　　　　　　　　　　p.93 … 1. *C*　　2. *B*　　3. *D*　　4. *B*

《體育娛樂》

p.97 … 1. *B*　　2. *A*　　3. *C*　　4. *C*　p.99 … 1. *B*　　2. *A*
p.102 … 1. *C*　　2. *A*　　3. *A*　　　　　p.106 … 1. *C*
p.107 … 2. *C*　　3. *A*　　4. *D*　　　　　p.110 … 1. *B*　　2. *C*　　3. *A*
p.113 … 1. *A*　　2. *D*　　　　　　　　　　p.116 … 1. *D*　　2. *C*　　3. *C*　　4. *D*
p.121 … 1. *D*　　2. *D*　　3. *C*　　　　　p.123 … 1. *B*　　2. *A*
p.126 … 1. *C*　　2. *D*　　3. *C*　　　　　p.128 … 1. *C*　　2. *B*
p.131 … 1. *D*　　2. *C*　　3. *A*

《生活醫藥》

p.135 … 1. *D*	2. *D*	
p.141 … 1. *C*	2. *D*	3. *A*
p.149 … 1. *B*	2. *B*	3. *C*
p.155 … 1. *A*	2. *D*	3. *B*
p.159 … 2. *C*	3. *D*	4. *A*
p.165 … 1. *D*	2. *B*	3. *C* 4. *A*

p.138 … 1. *C*	2. *B*	3. *D*	
p.144 … 1. *C*	2. *B*	3. *D*	
p.152 … 1. *C*	2. *D*	3. *B*	
p.158 … 1. *D*			
p.162 … 1. *D*	2. *D*	3. *D*	4. *A*
p.167 … *D*			

《經濟貿易》

p.171 … 1. *B*	2. *C*	3. *A*	4. *D*
p.176 … 1. *B*	2. *A*	3. *C*	4. *B*
p.184 … 1. *A*	2. *B*	3. *C*	
p.190 … 1. *C*	2. *B*	3. *C*	
p.198 … 1. *A*	2. *B*	3. *C*	4. *B*
p.204 … 1. *D*	2. *B*		

p.173 … *B*			
p.181 … 1. *A*	2. *D*		
p.187 … 1. *A*	2. *D*	3. *A*	
p.195 … 1. *D*	2. *C*	3. *C*	
p.201 … 1. *D*	2. *B*	3. *C*	4. *C*
p.207 … 1. *D*	2. *B*	3. *A*	

《社論專欄》

p.211 … 1. *D*	2. *D*	
p.216 … *B*		
p.223 … 1. *A*	2. *D*	
p.229 … 1. *B*	2. *A*	3. *D*
p.236 … 1. *C*	2. *A*	

p.214 … 1. *A*	2. *A*		
p.219 … 1. *D*	2. *D*	3. *D*	
p.226 … 1. *B*	2. *D*		
p.233 … 1. *D*	2. *A*	3. *C*	4. *D*
p.239 … 1. *B*	2. *D*	3. *C*	4. *C*

Editorial Staff

- **編著**/劉復苓
- **校訂**
  劉　毅・陳瑠琍・褚謙吉・謝静芳・蔡琇瑩
- **校閱**
  Ben Mayberry・Thomas Deneau・Thomas Ball
- **封面設計**/張鳳儀
- **版面設計**/張鳳儀・李碧芬
- **版面構成**/李碧芬・高文志
- **打字**
  黃淑貞・倪秀梅・吳秋香

||||||||||||||| ● 學習出版公司門市部 ● |||||||||||||||||

台北地區：台北市許昌街 10 號 2 樓 TEL：(02)2331-4060・2331-9209
台中地區：台中市綠川東街 32 號 8 樓 23 室
　　　　　TEL：(04)2223-2838

|||||||||||||||||||||||||||||||||||||||||||||||||||||

如何看懂 China Post & China News

編　　著／劉　復　苓
發　行　所／學習出版有限公司　　　　☎ (02) 2704-5525
郵 撥 帳 號／0512727-2 學習出版社帳戶
登　記　證／局版台業 2179 號
印　刷　所／裕強彩色印刷有限公司
台 北 門 市／台北市許昌街 10 號 2 F　　☎ (02) 2331-4060・2331-9209
台 中 門 市／台中市綠川東街 32 號 8 F 23 室　☎ (04) 2223-2838
台灣總經銷／紅螞蟻圖書有限公司　　　☎ (02) 2799-9490・2657-0132
美國總經銷／Evergreen Book Store　　☎ (818) 2813622

售價：新台幣一百八十元正

2001 年 11 月 1 日一版六刷